Contemporary Anthropology of Religion

*A series published with the Society for the
Anthropology of Religion*

Laurel Kendall, Series Editor
Curator, Division of Anthropology, America Museum
of Natural History

Published by Palgrave Macmillan:

Body / Meaning / Healing
By Thomas J. Csordas

*The Weight of the Past: Living with History in Mahajanga,
Madagascar*
By Michael Lambek

*After the Rescue: Jewish Identity and Community in
Contemporary Denmark*
By Andrew Buckser

Empowering the Past, Confronting the Future
By Andrew Strathern and Pamela J. Stewart

Islam Obscured: The Rhetoric of Anthropological Representation
By Daniel Martin Varisco

*Islam, Memory, and Morality in Yemen: Ruling
Families in Transition*
By Gabrielle Vom Bruck

*A Peaceful Jihad: Negotiating Identity and Modernity
in Muslim Java*
By Ronald Lukens-Bull

The Road to Clarity: Seventh-Day Adventism in Madagascar
By Eva Keller

Yoruba in Diaspora: An African Church in London
By Hermione Harris

*Islamic Narrative and Authority in Southeast Asia: From the
16th to the 21st Century*
By Thomas Gibson

Evangelicalism and Conflict in Northern Ireland
By Gladys Ganiel

*Christianity in the Local Context: Southern Baptists
in the Philippines*
By Brian M. Howell

*Missions and Conversions: Creating the Montagnard-Dega
Refugee Community*
By Thomas Pearson

*Gender, Catholicism, and Morality in Brazil: Virtuous Husbands,
Powerful Wives*
By Maya Mayblin

Direct Sales and Direct Faith in Latin America
By Peter S. Cahn

*Shamans, Spirituality, and Cultural Revitalization:
Explorations in Siberia and Beyond*
By Marjorie Mandelstam Balzer

*Spirits without Borders:
Vietnamese Spirit Mediums in a Transnational Age*
Karen Fjelstad and Nguyễn Thị Hiền

The Halal Frontier: Muslim Consumers in a Globalized Market
By Johan Fischer

The Halal Frontier

Muslim Consumers in a Globalized Market

Johan Fischer

First published in 2011 by
PALGRAVE MACMILLAN®
in the United States—a division of St. Martin's Press LLC,
175 Fifth Avenue, New York, NY 10010.

Where this book is distributed in the UK, Europe and the rest of the world,
this is by Palgrave Macmillan, a division of Macmillan Publishers Limited,
registered in England, company number 785998, of Houndmills,
Basingstoke, Hampshire RG21 6XS.

Palgrave Macmillan is the global academic imprint of the above companies
and has companies and representatives throughout the world.

Palgrave® and Macmillan® are registered trademarks in the United States,
the United Kingdom, Europe and other countries.

ISBN: 978–0–230–11418–0 (paperback)
ISBN: 978–0–230–11417–3 (hardcover)

Library of Congress Cataloging-in-Publication Data

Fischer, Johan.
    The halal frontier : Muslim consumers in a globalized market / Johan
Fischer.
        p. cm.—(Contemporary anthropology of religion)
    Includes bibliographical references and index.
        ISBN 978–0–230–11417–3 (hardcover)—ISBN 978–0–230–11418–0
(trade pbk.)
        1. Muslims—Dietary laws. 2. Halal food industry. 3. Food—Religious
aspects—Islam. 4. Halal food industry—Malaysia. 5. Theological
anthropology—Islam. I. Title. II. Series.

BP184.D5F57 2011
297.5'76—dc22   2010048082

A catalogue record of the book is available from the British Library.

Design by Newgen Imaging Systems (P) Ltd., Chennai, India.

First edition: July 2011

To Pernille, Anton, and Oscar

Previous Publications

Proper Islamic Consumption: Shopping among the Malays in Modern Malaysia. 2008.

Contents

Figures

Acknowledgments

Most of all, I would like to thank my Malay informants in London for their willingness to participate in and patience with my exploration of halal in their everyday lives. I would also like to extend my gratitude to Malaysian organizations and restaurants in London that were most helpful during my fieldwork.

In London, I was attached to the Department of Anthropology at Goldsmiths College, University of London. I am most grateful for the encouragement I received from staff during that time, and in particular, I would like to thank Sophie Day for making this affiliation possible and Keith Hart for valuable advice on the project.

In the Department of Society and Globalization at Roskilde University, I would like to thank Inge Jensen for helping out with the practicalities of the project. I would like to thank Christian Lund and Daniel Fleming for offering helpful input on writing up this research proposal for the Danish Council for Independent Research in Social Science that funded this project. I am most grateful for the help and support of the council.

I am indebted to Thomas Blom Hansen and Faisal Devji for their comments that helped this book come into being.

A special thanks goes to Laurel Kendall, Series Editor for Palgrave's Contemporary Anthropology of Religion series. Laurel has encouraged this project throughout and offered extremely detailed, constructive, and thoughtful advice and comments on many versions of the manuscript.

Finally, I would like to thank my wife, Pernille, and son Anton for enduring my absences during extended periods of fieldwork.

Glossary of Foreign Terms Used

This glossary includes local terms in the mother tongue of the Malays, *Bahasa Malaysia*, as well as foreign terms in Arabic

bumiputera	literally, "sons of the soil"
dakwah	literally, "invitation to salvation"
dhabh	ritual slaughtering
fatwa	opinion concerning Islamic law issued by an Islamic scholar
hadith	traditions concerning the life and works of the Prophet Muhammad
Hari Raya	a Muslim celebration that signifies the end of the fasting season of Ramadan
imam	a Muslim man who leads the prayers in a mosque
kelas pertengahan	middle class
lepak	loitering
makruh	detestable
mashbooh	doubtful
Melayu Baru	New Malay
najis	filth
salat	prayer times
shafi'i	the school of Islamic jurisprudence in Malaysia
sharia	Islamic law
surau	prayer house
tudung	long headscarf
ulama	literally, "those who know the law"
ummah	the community of Muslims
ustaz	religious teacher

Abbreviations and Acronyms

ABIM	Angkatan Belia Islam Malaysia or the Islamic Youth Movement of Malaysia
BMCC	British Malaysian Chamber of Commerce
BSE	Bovine Spongiform Encephalopathy
GMO	Genetically Modified Organisms
HDC	Halal Industry Development Corporation
HFA	Halal Food Authority
HMC	Halal Monitoring Committee
ICT	Information and Communication Technologies
IFANCA	Islamic Food and Nutrition Council of America
JAKIM	Jabatan Kemajuan Islam Malaysia or Islamic Development Department of Malaysia
MAFF	Ministry of Agriculture, Fisheries and Food
MATRADE	Malaysia External Trade Development Corporation
MCB	Muslim Council of Britain
MIHAS	Malaysia International Halal Showcase
NEP	New Economic Policy
NGO	Nongovernmental Organization
PAS	Parti Islam SeMalaysia
RM	Malaysian Ringgit
SIRIM	Standards and Industrial Research Institute of Malaysia
UMNO	United Malays National Organisation
WFM	World Food Market

Chapter 1

The Halal Frontier

Halal is an Arabic word that literally means "permissible" or "lawful." Conventionally, halal signifies "pure food" with regard to meat in particular by proper Islamic practice such as ritual slaughter and pork avoidance. In the modern world, halal is no longer an expression of esoteric forms of production, trade, and consumption but part of a huge and expanding globalized market. This book explores modern forms of halal understanding and practice among Malay Muslims in London, that is, the halal consumption of middle-class Malays in the diaspora. The connection between London, Malaysia, and Malays is no accident.

On August 16, 2004, Malaysia's prime minister, Abdullah Haji Ahmad Badawi, officially launched the first Malaysia International Halal Showcase (MIHAS) in the capital of Malaysia, Kuala Lumpur. The title of the prime minister's speech was "Window to the Global Halal Network" (http://mymall.netbuilder.com.my/index.php?doit =showclass&cid=36&domain=ehalal). He argued that establishing Malaysia as a "global halal hub" was a major priority for the government, and that MIHAS was the largest halal trade fair to be held anywhere in the world. Badawi asserted that halal products are increasingly being recognized by Muslims as well as non-Muslims globally as clean and safe in an era of diseases and "health disasters" due to "unhealthy practices." MIHAS also included a large number of product demonstrations and samples. These product demonstrations testified to the fact that, in Malaysia, halal has also proliferated into a wide range of nonfood products (toiletries, medication, and health products) as well as into services such as banking, insurance, education, and certification of halal. The global trend in recent years is to see that a thriving business in Islamic goods and services has emerged. Britain in particular was put forward as a highly lucrative market for halal. The global halal trade annually amounts to US$150 billion, and it is growing among the world's approximately 1.3 billion Muslims (Agriculture and Agri-Food Canada 2006).

This book explores the penetration of halal as a localized Malaysian practice by capitalism and how halal promotes Malay Muslim and ethnic identities. A central question is the Malaysian state's efforts to develop and dominate a global market in halal commodities and how Malays in London respond to and are affected by this effort. A plethora of halal commodities and discourses meets in London and filters into the everyday understandings, practices, and contestations of halal among middle-class Malays in the diaspora.

In his speech, Badawi stressed that the vast majority of the population in Malaysia consumes halal on a daily basis. The self-assuredness of this statement can be ascribed to the fact that the state in Malaysia has systematically regulated halal production, trade, and consumption since the early 1980s. Malaysian state bodies such as Jabatan Kemajuan Islam Malaysia or the Islamic Development Department of Malaysia (in English) (JAKIM)[1] regulates halal in the interfaces between Islamic revivalism, the state, and consumer culture.

In November 2005, the first Halal Exhibition at the major World Food Market (WFM) was held in London. The venue was ExCeL London. ExCeL London is a major exhibition and conference center in Docklands, an area in the southeastern part of the city that has been redeveloped principally for commercial and residential use.

The organizers of the WFM promoted it as Britain's largest trade fair for "ethnic" or "world food" products. In addition to the large number of booths displaying halal products, WFM also offered seminars on the business potential of halal in the rapidly expanding market. The Halal Exhibition also presents a whole range of new products, such as halal chocolate and toothpaste.

In 2006, a delegation from the Malaysia External Trade Development Corporation (MATRADE), Malaysia's national trade

Figure 1.1   The Malaysia External Trade Development Corporation booth at World Food Market

promotion agency, had a booth at the Halal Exhibition for the first time (figure 1.1).

A heading in a MATRADE advertisement in the WFM Official Show Guide read, "Malaysia. Your Reliable Trading Partner." The advertisement argued that

> Malaysia is among the world's top 20 trading nations and offers the international community a variety of world class products from sectors such as electrical and electronic, food, textiles and apparel, fur-

niture, wood, palm oil and rubber. Malaysia is the premier hub for the production and supply of quality halal products and services. The Malaysian halal logo is globally accepted and internationally recognized health and safety standards. [*sic*] (World Food Market 2006: inner sleeve and 27)

The advertisement presented samples of Malaysian halal products as well as a view over the modern and bustling city of Kuala Lumpur.

Malaysia holds a unique position in the global halal market. In the eyes of the MATRADE delegation at the Halal Exhibition, Britain, and London in particular, are potentially extremely lucrative markets. The Malaysian state's vision is to export its state-driven halal model to the emerging, but highly fragmented and complex, halal market in Britain. For that purpose, being represented at the WFM is essential.

The concept of a "frontier" refers to different arguments presented in the chapters to come. I am inspired by Edmund Leach's understandings of the frontier in his work on the highlands of Burma. In this study the frontier is described as "a border zone through which cultures interpenetrate in a dynamic manner" (Leach 1960: 50). The frontier concept informs central themes in the subsequent chapters.

A frontier is a space of progress and opportunity in which pioneers and entrepreneurs can cultivate their business visions and prosper. The Malaysian state's vision to export its national model of halal is a bid to cultivate and civilize London as a "wilderness" in which halal production, trade, certification, and consumption are seen as chaotic, disorderly, and undeveloped. Cultivating the wilderness signifies a new era for the *ummah* (the community of Muslims), now reconceptualized as ethical Muslim producers, traders, and consumers, as well as the revival of the golden past of Islamic trade networks.

What is more, the proliferation of halal in London is pushing and challenging the frontier between "the secular" and secular government, on the one hand, and religion, on the other hand. During fieldwork in London in 2006, powerful political discourses identified the veiling of Muslim women as an undesirable Islamic practice in public life. Many Muslims responded by arguing that, in the case of political discourses on dress, "rolling back the frontiers of government" was necessary. Ironically, many Muslims in Britain argue that the frontiers of government should be "rolled forward" to protect consumers in the expanding halal market.

The "halal frontier," understood as a "frontier of knowledge," I take to mean two things. First, it sheds light on a relatively unexplored subject. Second, the phrase a "frontier of knowledge" indicates that a better understanding of halal materiality is required. More specifically, I will investigate "cultivated" or "civilized" surfaces of halal commodities against their intrinsic or inner "wilderness." In doing so, I draw attention to the fact that, as more and more types of halal certification, and thus logos on halal products, appear in the halal market, in the eyes of many Muslim consumers this marking tells them relatively little about the actual or intrinsic halalness of the product. Thus, context, marking, and handling are reconceptualizing halal.

The concept of a frontier may also evoke ideas of an "urban frontier"—a jungle of complexity outside the direct control of ordered and organized centers of society. As halal proliferates, it moves frontiers and contributes to new forms of space making, thus lifting halal out of its base in halal butcher shops into public space, advertisements, and hypermarkets.

My use of "frontier" is "etic" in nature, that is, I apply this term as an outside observer, and my Malay informants do not specifically use the word "frontier" as a local or "emic" category.

The research question I answer in this book is this: how is Malay middle-class consumption of halal in the diaspora taking place between globalized markets, Malaysian sentiments, and Islam? In other words, it argues that the proliferation of modern halal is entangled in evermore-complex webs of political, economic, religious, ethnic, and national significance. I explore how this is happening through particular understandings and practices of halal in a local context as part of transformed global markets of religious mass consumption. The focus is on how Malay diasporic groups on "the frontier" consume and respond to halal in the interfaces between powerful discourses in Malaysia and beyond that promote and brand halal products as proper consumption and the state as well as Islamic organizations in Britain. Closely related to this, an important issue is the ambiguity that arises when middle-class Malays are simultaneously called upon by the above discourses, on the one hand, to practice pious halal consumption and, on the other hand, to embody pragmatism and flexibility as a modern Muslim diasporic group "on the frontier." As we shall see, much of this confusion arises from the pluralization of everyday consumer choices these Malays experience in London.

Currently, religion and food are being linked and reconfigured in novel ways, and these transformations (e.g., related to globalization, spirituality, nutrition, distinctions, politics, and identities) call for renewed attention from the perspective of the anthropology of religion.

What Is Halal?

Halal literally means "lawful" or "permitted." The Koran and the Sunna (the life, actions, and teachings of the Prophet Muhammad) exhort Muslims to eat the good and lawful food God has provided for them, but a number of conditions and prohibitions are observed. Muslims are expressly forbidden from consuming carrion, spurting blood, pork, and foods that have been consecrated to any being other than God himself. These substances are haram ("unlawful" or "forbidden").[2] The lawfulness of meat depends on how it is obtained. Ritual slaughtering, *dhabh*, entails that the animal is killed in God's name by making a fatal incision across the throat. In this process, the blood should be drained out as fully as possible. Among Muslim groups and individuals, the question of the stunning of animals prior to slaughter is highly contested, that is, some Muslims consider only meat from unstunned animals halal, whereas others accept that stunning is part of modern and ethical food production.

Sea creatures and locusts are considered halal. Because the sea is seen to be pure in essence, all marine animals, even if they have died spontaneously, are halal. Despite the fact that they are not mentioned in the Koran, land creatures such as predators, dogs, and, in the eyes of some jurists, donkeys are haram. What is more, crocodiles, weasels, pelicans, otters, foxes, elephants, ravens, and insects have been condemned by the *ulama* (literally, those who know the law or religious scholars). Often some of these animals are seen as *makruh* or detestable and thus not haram (Denny 2006: 278). Divergences between jurists of the different schools of Islamic jurisprudence (Hanafi, Maliki, Hanbali, and *Shafi'i*, which is the school of thought dominant in Malaysia) on halal understanding and practice exist.

Another significant Islamic prohibition relates to wine and any other alcoholic drink or substance, all of which are haram, whatever the quantity or substance (Denny 2006: 279).

With the advent of Islam, ancient negative attitudes toward pigs and pork were reinforced. Inspired by Jewish law, the Prophet Mohammad banned the flesh of pigs as the only animal to be prohibited, and in the Koran, the ban is repeated several times (Simoons 1994: 32). In effect, Muslims were distinguished from their Christian adversaries (Simoons 1994: 33). Some Muslim groups came to abhor pigs and pork to such an extent that everything touched by them was regarded as contaminated and worthless (Simoons 1994: 33). Under Western colonialism, pig abhorrence declined in many parts of the world, only to increase again with the end of European colonial rule after World War II, and especially with Islamic revivalism (Simoons 1994: 36). Historically, it was Arab traders who spread Islam in peninsular Malaysia in the thirteenth century, leading to a considerable reduction in keeping pigs and eating pork in this region (Simoons 1994: 58).

The reasons for the ban on pork within Islam largely follow the five main types of explanation advanced to analyze the origin of the Hebrew food laws. One is that these are arbitrary and make no sense to humans and can only be understood by God. Another is that injunctions were based on sanitary concerns (Simoons 1994). A symbolic explanation proposed by Mary Douglas (see below) argues that acceptable animals represented proper human behavior versus the sinful behavior of banned animals. Yet another explanation is that Hebrew food laws originated in their rejections of cultic practices of alien peoples and of the worship of deities other than Jehovah. Involved in both the third and fourth hypotheses is the notion that the Hebrews wanted to set themselves apart from other peoples. Some anthropologists, most famously Marvin Harris, have argued for a fifth and recent explanation, according to which the prohibitions are grounded in economic, environmental, and/or ecological reasons (Simoons 1994: 64–65). According to Marvin Harris (1977,

1998) with the rise of Islam, the Israelite taboo on pigs was reconceptualized as a new set of sanctioned dietary laws "ecological" in
essence, that is, religious ideas is traced to the cost/benefit of ecological processes.

The proliferation of halal can be seen as distinct sets of invocations
of haram or taboo. Taboo can protect distinctive categories of the
universe, consensus, and certainty about the organization of the cos-
mos, thus reducing intellectual and social disorder (Douglas 2004:
xi). However, certainty and order easily mirror feelings of uncertainty
and disorder. These doubts mostly surface in everyday strategies
about how to go about practicing ever-intensifying demands for the
Islamically proper in consumption. Elsewhere, Douglas (1975: 275)
argues that when people become aware of encroachment and danger,
dietary rules that control what goes into the body function as an anal-
ogy of the corpus of their cultural categories at risk.

To many people, including my Malay middle-class informants on
the frontier, meat is synonymous with "real" food (Fiddes 1991: 14),
but at the same time, it is mostly particular types of meat that are
taboo. Meat is often considered prestigious and vital for nutrition, on
the one hand, and dangerously immoral and potentially unhealthy,
on the other hand (Fiddes 1991: 2). During fieldwork in London, I
realized that none of my informants were vegetarians. In the eyes of
informants, a "proper" meal includes meat of some kind.

The debate over the origins of the ban on pork in Judaism and Islam
is far from resolved, and one central reason for this is that there is not
sufficient historical evidence in existence. The prohibition of pork is
one of the rare food taboos that live on in Islam, but the true reason
for its prohibition is unknown. My brief discussion of anthropologists
Douglas and Harris's arguments serves the purpose of providing the
reader with key arguments in a debate that has spanned decades and
that still seems to inform scholarly and popular controversy over not
only the prohibition of pork but also the nature of taboo itself.

In my exploration of the proliferation of halal, I am inspired by
Rouse and Hoskins's (2004) analysis of soul food, the traditional
food of black Americans of the South, in contemporary United
States. Halal brings together a range of political and historical
controversies (Hoskins and Rouse 2004: 230). Moreover, classical

anthropological concerns with food taboos can be opened up to history and ways in which the experience of the past is reinterpreted in terms of struggles of the present (Hoskins and Rouse 2004: 230). The study of soul food investigates how complex societies and contemporary movements are not immune to processes of classification but incorporate them into new visions of purity (Rouse and Hoskins 2004: 230). There seems to be contextual/temporal dimensions to ideas of purity and impurity (Rouse and Hoskins 2004: 235). The ban on eating pork "organizes multiple political, social, and personal locations, and these food categories shift in priority based upon changing spatial and ideological contexts" (Rouse and Hoskins 2004: 237). The authors show that halal is part of "a communicative process of social action, in which pragmatic and social dimensions are fused to comment on a particular historical moment" (Rouse and Hoskins 2004: 227). Furthermore, halal signifies practices that can be associated with race, authenticity, group membership, and citizenship. In all these, the preparation and exchange of food are essential communicative processes (Rouse and Hoskins 2004: 228). I agree that theories of taboo often tend to be smooth, functional, and strangely disembedded in terms of temporal and spatial context, and Rouse and Hoskins's study forcefully demonstrates the importance of ethnographic substantiation. The global era, for example, presents novel conditions for the mass production, marketing, and consumption of halal.

Among urban Muslims in China, the Hui, halal food and eating stood out as the most important identity marker in contradistinction to the surrounding Han majority. Besides nutritional and economic functions, food and eating practices expressed values and traits that they regarded as fundamentally Hui (Gillette 2000: 114). The food taboo was formative of ethnic and religious distinctions (Gillette 2000: 121), and to Hui, pigs were dirty not only because they were unsanitary but also because of their nature (Gillette 2000: 119).

In a Southeast Asian context, taboos distinguish between groups and individuals within their own society. Moreover, taboos operate in terms of the production, preparation, and distribution of food (Manderson 1986a: 10). In modern Singapore, many Malays are fastidious about halal, but they practice this fastidiousness pragmatically in the context of the ethnic Chinese majority (Nasir, Pereira, and Turner 2009).

However, modern halal cannot be understood simply as part of a stable taxonomy. In addition to halal and haram, doubtful things should be avoided, that is, there is a gray area between the clearly lawful and the unlawful (Riaz and Chaudry 2004: 6–7). The doubtful or questionable is expressed in the word *mashbooh* (Riaz and Chaudry 2004: 7), which can be evoked by divergences in religious scholars' opinions or the suspicion of undetermined or prohibited ingredients in a commodity. Hence, far more abstract, individual, and fuzzy aspects of context and handling are involved in determining the halalness of a product. The interpretation of these *mashbooh* areas is left open to Islamic specialists and state institutions such as JAKIM and local Islamic organizations in London. To determine whether a foodstuff is halal or haram "depends on its nature, how it is processed, and how it is obtained" (Riaz and Chaudry 2004: 14). In the end, however, the underlying principle behind the prohibitions remains "divine order" (Riaz and Chaudry 2004: 12).

Muslim dietary rules assumed new significance in the twentieth century, as some Muslims began striving to demonstrate how such rules conform to modern reason and the findings of scientific research. Another common theme in the revival and renewal of these dietary rules seems to be the search for alternatives to what are seen to be Western values, ideologies, and lifestyles. These reevaluations of requirements and prohibitions are prominent, first, in postcolonial Islamic cultures such as Malaysia and, second, among diasporic groups for whom halal can serve as a focal point for Islamic movements and identities (Esposito 1995: 376).

For example, some Turkish migrants in Germany take great care to prevent moral contamination from haram meat that can seem threatening to them. These concerns have moved to the forefront in the diaspora, whereas these dietary laws are "nearly unconscious" in Turkey (Mandel 1996: 151). Similarly, in the eyes of Somalis in Toronto and London, halal is an important question in everyday life (McGown 1999). In Toronto, one of McGown's informants goes to Kentucky Fried Chicken and Burger King, whereas McDonald's is avoided because he suspects lard is used for frying French fries.

Similarly, toothpaste was suspected of containing lard (McGown 1999: 74).

Conversely, dietary laws among urban Malay Muslims in Malaysia are highly conscious, and halal is ubiquitous among them as a signifier in public as well as in private spaces or domains. During fieldwork in 2009–2010, I found that state halal certified that Colgate toothpaste and Coca-Cola (figure 1.2) were ubiquitous in supermarkets in Kuala Lumpur. The question I will answer is how these sentiments are translated into halal understanding and practice in a diasporic context on the frontier.

In the modern food industry around the world, a number of Muslim requirements have taken effect, such as an injunction to avoid any substances that may be contaminated with porcine residues or alcohol, such as gelatin, glycerin, emulsifiers, enzymes, flavors, and

Figure 1.2   Halal Coca-Cola certified by the Malaysian state. The Malaysian state's halal logo issued by JAKIM displays in Arabic the word "halal" at the center and "Malaysia" at the bottom

flavorings (Riaz and Chaudry 2004: 22–25). An example of this is the headline of an article in the *Guardian* (October 26, 2006), one of Britain's large daily newspapers, reading "Something Fishy in Your Pasta?" The article demonstrated that in some cases, gelatin, among other things, is being "sneaked" into a variety of foods. The problem in certifying food and other products with regard to these substances is that they are extremely difficult to detect.

For some Muslims, halal sensibilities necessitate that halal products be produced by Muslims only and that this type of production be kept strictly separate from nonhalal production—not unlike the way in which the proliferation of rules and taboos concerning food in orthodox Judaism excludes others as "unclean."

Among some Malay Muslims in London, eating fast food at McDonald's is contested. Many Muslim groups wish to enjoy eating this type of food without going against their religious beliefs, but they may have reservations about the ingredients (Roy 2002: 31). Arguably, halal is not linked with a particular culture and could fit unproblematically with fast food and a global cuisine (Roy 2002). However, halal understanding and practice are premised on divergences between a plethora of Muslim groups and individuals. Thus, sociological explanations are not always tuned to capturing the everyday complexity involved in modern halal consumption. Hence, this book is an ethnographic exploration of halal on the halal frontier of London, but it also addresses a number of issues global in scope.

The Globalization of a Religious Market

In this multisited study, I have followed middle-class Malays from Malaysia and halal commodities (food and nonfood) from the perspective of the anthropology of religion. Halal in London signifies intensified global flows of commodities as well as mass consumption and marketing. I examine how halal is transformed from being an expression of esoteric forms of production, trade, and consumption to become part of a huge and expanding globalized market. This section argues that contemporary reconfigurations of the relationship between religion and food in a globalized world are important to modern halal understanding and practice. Halal with respect to meat in particular has engaged and intrigued the discipline of anthropology in the past. However, the contemporary proliferation of modern halal on a global scale has not attracted systematic anthropological attention. This book explores the commercialization of halal for a global market, that is, the kinds of social, moral, hygienic, and economic issues that come to the fore as middle-class Malays engage in halal in contemporary London.

Of course, anthropological interest in the relationship between religion and food is extensive. Claude Lévi-Strauss (1968: 87) argued that exploring food could generate "a significant knowledge of the unconscious attitudes of the society or societies under consideration." The underlying logic in this type of analysis is that religion, on the one hand, and dietary understandings and practices, on the other hand, are inseparable forces shaping human cosmology. In seminal studies of food and religion/cosmology by Lévi-Strauss (1968), Emile Durkheim (1995), and Mary Douglas (1972, 1975, 2004), binaries such as edible/inedible, sacred/profane, and raw/cooked are vital. Barthes (1975: 72) writes that "to eat is a behavior that develops beyond its own ends, replacing, summing up, and signaling other behaviors, and it is precisely for these reasons that it is a sign." (1975: 72). Food is a sign vital to individual, group, and national identities. Simultaneously, basic food taxonomies "incorporate the individual into the group" and "situate the whole group in relation to the universe" (Barthes 1975: 172). I review a few of these seminal studies of food in the anthropology of religion above to draw attention to the fact that few of these anthropologists could have anticipated the emergence of a global market for halal.

The proliferation of halal applies to what Lee (1993) from a sociological perspective has called the globalization of religious markets. He writes that rules and understandings for the attainment of salvation "have become important commodities in an expanding religious market that transcends international boundaries" (Lee 1993: 36). Politicians, bureaucrats, and entrepreneurs use the popular mass media to manipulate popular wants (Lee 1993: 37). More specifically, the global proliferation of halal is advertised as religious needs that fulfill private desires such as piety, purity, and health—all intimately linked to the "market for identities" (Navaro-Yashin 2002: 11) and "contingent relations of the global marketplace" (Devji 2005: 11). Planners of a religious economy try to package "convincing soteriologies and devise practical means of delivery for their target populations in order to achieve popularity, maintain or advance a religious vision, legitimate a political hegemony, or simply gain wealth" (Lee 1993: 48). However, such sociological assumptions about the globalization of religious markets warrant empirical substantiation.

Modern and global halal can be a sign of both "nutrition" and "spirituality" (Coveney 2000). For modern consumers, "nutrition" functions as both a scientific and a spiritual/ethical discipline. Nutrition serves this dual function by providing a range of scientific knowledges about food and the body as "spiritual" disciplines: "'Spiritual' here does not necessarily equate with 'theological' but refers to the means by which individuals are required to construct themselves with a 'correct' concern for the 'proper' way of behaving in relation to eating" (Coveney 2000: xvi). What is more, subjects of modern dietary science are suffused with ethical and "spiritual" problems in the form of government of food choice: "The ethics of nutrition might not be explicitly 'divine,' but it is spiritual and it is sober" (Coveney 2000: 161).

In the proliferation of modern halal, powerful discourses overlap. Malays in London are exposed to such discourses that attempt to discipline consumption, patrol, and push the borders between taxonomical entities such as edible/inedible in an expanding global food market. The effects of these entangled discourses on everyday Malay Muslim consumption seem to be reinforced in a diasporic context. Among Malays in London, knowledge of food conditions such distinctions. To understand halal as a particular form of (food) consumption, I show that "national, regional, linguistic and religious distinctions are often marked in culinary fashions" (Caplan 1997: 13).

An important topic is that the politics of food has an effect on religious groups. Although the state increasingly regulates the food market in an EU membership country such as Britain, this is not the case with "ethnic," "spiritual," "world," or "religious" food/cuisines, be it ayurveda, feng shui, kosher, or halal. Religious food and markets are mostly outside direct consumer protection and state regulation.

Only recently, food has emerged as a highly political topic connecting "individual bodies to abstract communities and techno scientific innovations to moral concerns" (Lien 2004: 1). The politics of food is intimately linked to global flows of religious goods. Moreover, food scares concerning Bovine Spongiform Encephalopathy (BSE) and salmonella, on the one hand, and Genetically Modified Organisms (GMO), on the other, pose new ethical questions in the interfaces among state politics, markets, and religious/ethical stances. Such issues require that notions of politics be expanded to cover fields that are not conventionally considered "political" (Lien 2004: 2. For example, halal in a country such as Britain is essentially outside direct state regulation, and these issues are linked to religious consumption and "the secular."

The politics of food is also politics at a distance in a diasporic context. The recent intensification of the "delocalization" of food, that is, the potential impact of local events on distant affairs (Lien 2004: 4), is clear in the case of the proliferation of halal.

An example of this was a major food scandal in Indonesia in 2001 that triggered a new phase of halal proliferation on a global scale to cover areas such as enzyme production. The Majelis Ulama Indonesia or Indonesian Ulemas Council (in English), set up by the Indonesian state in 1975, accused a Japanese company of using pork products in the production of the flavor enhancer monosodium glutamate and demanded that the Indonesian government take appropriate action. It was a serious accusation: if true, the company would have violated halal rules, which forbid Muslims from eating any pork or pork-derived products.

As a consequence of the scandal, several of the company's employees were arrested, and a public apology was issued. It is most likely that the flavor enhancer did not contain any pork products; instead, the company conceded to having replaced a beef derivative with the pork derivative bactosoytone in the production process, for economic reasons. Bactosoytone was used as a medium to cultivate bacteria that produce the enzymes necessary to make monosodium glutamate. As the products of the company had previously been certified as halal by the Majelis Ulama Indonesia, the scandal seemed to undermine or question the legitimacy of these religious scholars in the eyes of millions of Muslim consumers. The scandal also made it clear that even multinational companies can come into conflict with the rising number of Muslim consumers and organizations if they overlook or disregard religiously inspired customs.

Indeed, the Indonesian scandal triggered similar enquiries at other companies worldwide. For example, Novozymes, a company that specializes in producing enzymes for a wide range of applications, including scientific research and food processing, was one of these. Customers of Novozymes became more aware of the validity of halal certifications, and the company eventually chose to have its products certified by the Islamic Food and Nutrition Council of America (IFANCA), a major halal certifying body, which together with JAKIM is one of the world's largest certifiers. Around that time, many other food and pharmaceutical companies, including Nestlé, as we shall see in detail, also decided to have their products certified as halal by various Muslim organizations.[3]

Hence,

> as food systems are globalized, food becomes entangled in complex webs of political significance....it vastly increases the number of diverse interests, relations and regulatory frameworks that are enrolled as each food item makes its way from production to consumption. (Lien 2004: 4)

Halal sits uneasily between such globalized food systems, complex webs of political/national significance, and (insufficient) regulatory frameworks.

The globalization of the agrifood system has produced a "complexification" of food supply similar to what we have seen in other commodities (Busch 2004: 170). Consequently, a food market such as that of Britain and London has witnessed complexification and pluralization of food choices, and that effect is also evident with halal that today applies to much more than locally slaughtered meat.

Anthropologists studying food as a "sign" or "code" as it were in local contexts have long acknowledged that food and eating also involve political economy at different levels of the social scale such as households, states, and their formation and structure (Goody 1982). Along the same lines, I argue that under globalization, these processes are intensifying and that halal understanding and practice in

a local context should also be explored within a framework of political economy. Another important insight is that with regard to food,
"global capitalism today has made peace with cultural diversity" (Wilk
2006: 197). An example of this is Nestlé's recent interest in halal that
was hyped during my fieldwork in 2006.

In recent years, a wave of popular literature and other media products have promoted such religious markets—in terms of food often
as "spiritual" or "world" cuisines. I provide a few examples of these
popular sources, but I will not discuss the large bodies of scholarly
literature that also explore these trends. For ayurveda, the book *The
Ayurveda Encyclopedia: Natural Secrets to Healing, Prevention, and
Longevity* (Tirtha 2007) provides a good example. With regard to
kosher, the book *Kosher Living. It's More Than Just the Food* (Isaacs
2005) signifies this trend. *Feng Shui Food: Create Great Looking, Great
Tasting Food That Will Revolutionize Your Meals and Revitalize Your
Life* (Brown and Saunders 1999) similarly reflects these tendencies,
and finally, from a Christian perspective, food is placed in a larger
religious market and perspective: *Food for Life. The Spirituality and
Ethics of Eating* (Jung 2004). This book, it is argued, "will help people learn to enjoy their lives more—perhaps much more. Recognizing
the Goodness of God in our eating is one way to discover such delight
and joy" (Jung 2004: xi).

Although popular as well as scholarly sources on food/cuisines
and ayurveda, feng shui, kosher, and Christianity are in abundance,
to my knowledge the only pendant in English with regard to halal,
except for the halal handbooks by a Malaysian publisher discussed
below, is *Halal Food, Fun and Laughter* (Delgado 2005). The author
contends that

> this cookbook combines a winning "recipe" for a healthy lifestyle:
> good food, some fun and laughter and last but most importantly,
> remembrances of Allah, by adding some wonderful Qur'an and *hadith*
> [traditions concerning the life and works of the Prophet Muhammad]
> to the mix to help create a happier and healthier recipe for your life.
> (Delgado 2005: 1)

These cookbooks seem to evoke a form of cosmopolitan "cooking and
spirituality moment," that is, combining food, halal, and health with
a relaxed lifestyle. Comparing the feng shui cookbook, for example,

and *Halal Food, Fun and Laughter*, some differences emerge. The halal cookbook is more "textual" in its reference to Islamic sources, whereas the feng shui cookbook builds on more "spiritual" or "metaphysical" discourses, on the one hand, and presentation/appearance of food, on the other. Arguably, the ayurveda cookbook shares these tendencies. Comparing these cookbooks also draws attention to the fact that overwhelmingly it is kosher and halal products that can be certified.

I have argued that a range of broader transformations and processes global in scale links food and the fields of nutrition, spirituality, political economy, and globalized religious markets. These markets constitute a framework for ways in which halal is understood and practiced among middle-class Malays in London. At the same time, globalized religious markets are also markets for identities deserving attention from the perspective of anthropology of religion—for example, with regard to responses and pragmatism of religious consumers to the current delocalization and pluralization of shopping choices on a halal frontier such as London. In other words, everyday considerations that are not necessarily linked to religion, morality, or politics are important. Consequently, the determination of food consumption patterns is complex and negotiated balancing authority/affection, responsibility/desire to please, patterns of preference, mutual concern for one another's welfare, likes and dislikes, work load and pattern, and convenience and cost in terms of time and money (Caplan et al. 1998: 196). Ethnographic specificity is required to capture ways in which this complexity with regard to halal is played out in everyday life among middle-class Malays who migrated from Malaysia in London.

State, Market, and Malay Mobility

Although the state does not really interfere with halal in Britain, the Malaysian state is very much present in the everyday lives of Malay Muslims in Malaysia, as well as diasporic Malays in London. In fact, "Malaysian Islam is perhaps the most monolithic and most state-regulated" (Bakar 2008: 82). I shall return to this aspect in detail in Chapter 2. Here, it suffices to say that this point is important to

understand the relationship between Malaysia, the Malaysian state, Malays, and halal. Focusing on Malays in London, I shall show that understandings and practices of halal are incomprehensible without comparing Malaysia and Britain as two countries in which the state and its presence are a sign of quite different trajectories and meanings. A specific example of this is the way in which the Malaysian state has regulated halal in Malaysia since the 1980s.

This work can therefore be said to be a comparative anthropology of the state, that is, an exploration of Malay halal consumption practiced in the interfaces between two powerful "languages of stateness" (Hansen and Stepputat 2001: 37) in Malaysia and Britain, which help shape the state, governance, effects, and subjectivities. These diasporic Malays live at the margins of two states: in the case of Malaysian halal, sovereign power exercised by the state disciplines Muslim bodies, thus making modern forms of Islamic bureaucratization a sign of Malay ethnicity. However, in Britain, some Muslims and Islamic organizations call upon the state to help recognize and standardize halal.

The more the culture of Islamic consumption asserts itself, the more the state's incapacity to define what is legitimate halal and thus the unity of Islam is felt. Contrary to the intense debate in Britain over veiling (overt and on bodies), for example, there is no corresponding state discourse on halal (covert and in bodies). Hence, Malay diasporic groups' consumption and negotiation of halal takes place in the interfaces between powerful Malaysian state discourses, the state, and Islamic organizations in Britain and the global commercialization of halal that is intensifying.

Multinational companies now recognize halal as an important and profitable new market, and it is this fact that is also fueling the halal vision of the ethnicized state in Malaysia and of entrepreneurs linked directly or indirectly to it. According to the director of KasehDia, a Malaysian publishing company that produces *The Halal Journal: Business, Lifestyle, Trends,* the Malaysian state's focus on halal is finally being acknowledged by "industry giants" "confirming their positions in the halal market, with Nestlé, Tesco (a U.K.-based international grocery and merchandising retail chain. Tesco is the largest British retailer by both global sales and domestic market share) and McDonald's all playing leading roles" (Evans 2006: 25).

In June 2006, Tesco announced that it would be sourcing 1 billion Malaysian Ringgit (RM), about US$ 285,000,000, of certified halal products over the next five years to service selected U.K. stores (Evans 2006: 25). Thus, halal is being lifted out of its traditional base in local halal butcher's shops to become part of "world food" ranges in major supermarkets.

Only recently has the established concept of halal, which largely focuses on ritual slaughter and pork and alcohol avoidance, been resignified and assumed new meanings in terms of what is pure, sacred, appropriate, or healthy. A growing number of Muslim consumers are concerned not only with traditional halal food requirements in the Koran but also with contamination from haram sources in products such as toiletries and medication.

During a previous period of fieldwork in Malaysia, I noticed an advertisement in *The Star*, one of the major newspapers in English in Malaysia, dated May 2, 2002. The heading read, "Introducing Al Jaulah: Travel with Total Peace of Mind." The advertisement shows two young (presumably Malay) Muslim women in London. We see a distorted, unfocused, twisted image of Tower Bridge in the background adding to the impression that the Occidental setting is disturbing, to say the least. This eerie feeling demands the comfort of stabilizing Muslim-friendly services and activities on the trip. Traveling with Al Jaulah, the reader is guaranteed "meals prepared by local Muslim chefs. Flight Muslim meals...sightseeing, shopping, shops, and sights of Muslim interest in addition to other popular attractions."

A Nestlé advertisement in *The Halal Journal* (2010) shows a Muslim woman wearing a *tudung* (long headscarf) eating a KitKat chocolate bar in front of a computer in her office with London's Big Ben and Parliament in the background. The heading reads, "Bringing Peace of Mind around the World." The text states that

> "Halal" benefits everyone—in Malaysia and all over the world. Since the 1980s Nestlé Malaysia has been producing products according to guidelines on "Halal" practices and actively promoting "Halal" standards to both Muslim and non-Muslim consumers. We have earned the

recognition as the "Halal" Centre of excellence for the Nestlé Group worldwide. When you next enjoy your favourite Nestlé product, bear in mind you're joined by consumers who are enjoying the same with peace of mind in more than fifty countries around the world where our "Halal" products are available.

Following the text is a clear image of JAKIM's halal logo.

Hence, Britain is a tourist destination to Malays and Muslims more generally, and the country is also being targeted as a lucrative halal market in a plethora of halal discourses. What is more, Britain is an accommodating country in which entrepreneurial Muslims can work and prosper.

The main motive for focusing on Malays in multiethnic London is, first, that the Malaysian state's vision of and commitment to promoting halal specifically identifies London as a center for halal production, trade, and consumption. London is in many ways a focal point for most Muslims in the United Kingdom, and Edgware Road in the city center and Whitechapel Road in the East End, for example, are good examples of major changes and developments in the business and entrepreneurial environment in the city over the past decade or so. Most of the shops, kiosks, restaurants, cafes, money transfer agencies, barbers, and estate agencies in these areas are businesses with Muslim ethnic backgrounds. The proliferation of halal shops and other businesses in London "mirrors the wider growth of ethnic minority businesses in the UK. Many also see the increasing Muslim population in the UK and Europe as encouragement to invest in such businesses and industries" (Ahmed 2008: 655).

Second, London is home to a substantial number of Malays and Malaysian organizations such as United Malays National Organisation (UMNO), the dominant political party in Malaysia since independence from Britain in 1957, and MATRADE. Third, the focus on Malay halal consumption in London allows me to offer comparisons to my previous research on halal and consumption among Malay middle-class families in urban Malaysia. The halal market is rapidly expanding in London, and this is leading to a pluralization of this market, which Muslim consumers are faced with in their daily lives. For example, a central question among my Malay informants is this: does being fastidious about halal make you a better person or Muslim? This study also highlights some more general implications for the emergence of religious mass consumption in a global context.

The multiplicity and ambiguity involved in the processes of halal production, certification, marketing, and consumption is addressed in the handbook *Halal Food: A Guide to Good Eating—Kuala Lumpur* (Azmi 2003a) by the Malaysian publisher KasehDia. In the book, over a hundred restaurants, takeaway counters, and cafés in Kuala Lumpur are listed and reviewed. Much more than strictly traditional halal requirements are involved in guiding Muslim consumers: the spatial context (atmosphere/feel/ambience) of food consumption as practice may be just as significant as the intrinsic qualities of the food and its ingredients. The various establishments are classified according to their halalness, for example, whether alcohol is sold or food is produced and served by Muslims or non-Muslims. Explicitly, the authors state in the introduction that they are referring to and relying on the official channels of Malaysian halal certification and not on their personal preferences:

> Halal certification in Malaysia is given out by government agencies that is valid for one year. Our halal categories [classification of the different restaurants according to "halalness" in the book] are partly based on the classification by these agencies. If any of them retract the halal certification from any of the food outlets, the information in this book regarding the particular food outlet is considered null and void. (Azmi 2003a: IX)

All of this is expressive of new formations of meta-industries that are beyond the strictly religious focus on halal/haram dichotomies and halal certification, but instead target the marketing, pluralization, and promotion of halal as a brand or logo of Malaysian state capitalism.

In this publisher's pendant to the Kuala Lumpur guide, *Halal Food: A Guide to Good Eating—London*, the introduction states that

> the city of London does not have a specific all-encompassing authority that acts as the central or sole halal certifier for all restaurants. However, the city has several empowering bodies and councils who give certifications to food suppliers and outlets. (Azmi 2003b: 11)

The present book explores Malay understandings and practices of these divergent forms of certification as expressions of widely different contexts of politics, religion, and consumption. An important question is how the certification of these "empowering bodies" shapes the halal market in London.

In Malaysia, constitutionally Malays are only Malays if they are Muslims, speak the Malay language—*Bahasa Melayu* or Bahasa Malaysia—and follow Malay customs. Trying to talk of "the Malays" as a people is a subject matter fraught with diversity and contradiction, that is, who is "Malay" and what it means to be "Malay" are open questions (Milner 2008). I agree with the argument "to focus on 'Malayness' rather than on 'the Malays.' It makes sense to examine the development of an idea (or more accurately several ideas, and the contest around them) than to speak of the evolution of a people" (Milner 2008: 16). An ethnography of halal understanding and practice is one way of exploring modern forms of diasporic Malayness and its contestation.

Among the political elite in Malaysia, there exists a fascination with discovering or even inventing a "Malay diaspora." The particularity of this "diaspora-envy" is a sign of "modern Malay aspirations towards cosmopolitanism and 'global reach'" (Kessler 1999: 23). Kessler (1999: 34–35) relates an anecdote about a leading Malay publicist visiting London's Chinatown. The publicist asked,

> This is Chinatown, but where is Malaytown? Why are there no similar Malay communities here in London and elsewhere throughout the world that have the same relation to the *alam Melayu* [Malay world] that the world's Chinatowns have to the modern civilization of the old Middle Kingdom?

There is an almost mythical texture to Chinatown as an embodiment of Chinese trade networks. Accumulated money and mechanisms of trust within transnational trading networks give shape to such diasporic communities (Kessler 1999: 35).

I show that the proliferation of halal among middle-class Malays in London sits uneasily between two essential characteristics or dimensions of modern diasporas: an economic dimension linked to investment and trade and a future aspect to a large extent nourished by diasporic aspirations.

An example of the way in which diaspora is contested within the political field surfaced in a newspaper article in *The Star* dated May 13, 2006. In Malaysia, the higher education minister had insisted that students abroad should have "a strong sense of nationalism and patriotism, and should return home to serve the country after completing their studies." Many Malays in London are students (as we shall see many of my informants are students), and they are supported by the Malaysian state, and thus, the above debate was important for them as a diasporic group. Hence, the social formation of diaspora often "is best understood as composed of those who passionately share the conflicts that divide it about the nature of their local, national, and transnational commitments and identities" (Tölölyan 2000: 111).

What is more, "The globalization of production and consumption, or the heightened mobility of people, goods, ideas, and capital, also creates transnational communities" (Levitt 2001: 7–8). As we shall see, the state in Malaysia together with civic, religious, and political institutions create and reinforce transnationalism (Levitt 2001: 5). What Levitt has called transnational villages create and are themselves created by such political, religious, and civic organizations that work across borders meeting the needs of their transnational members who participate in both settings (Levitt 2001: 11–12). To sum up, I explore a hitherto insufficient focus on diasporas with regard to powerful linkages between "intellectual creativity, diasporic quotidian culture, subjective consciousness, and political action" (Werbner 2000: 5), as well as "the relation between aesthetic production, economic links, and political agendas" (Werbner 2000: 17).

A Note on Methodology

The fieldwork for this study has produced a multisited ethnography involving Kuala Lumpur and London. I conducted fieldwork for one month in Kuala Lumpur in connection with MIHAS 2006. Previously, I conducted fieldwork in Malaysia for a period of two years since 1996. Starting in 2005, I visited London on several occasions, for example, in connection with the Halal Exhibition at the WFM held in November 2005 and 2006. The extended period of fieldwork in London took place from July to December 2006, with shorter stays in 2007.

My methodology rests, first, on an intention to "follow the people" (Marcus 1995: 106), leading me to focus on descriptions of Malays who migrated from Kuala Lumpur to London and their migration narratives with special emphasis on understandings and practices of halal in these two locations. Second, I endeavored to "follow the thing," that is, to trace the circulation of halal commodities as manifestly material objects of study (Marcus 1995: 106). At the same time, commodities can be seen as "things with a particular type of social potential" (Appadurai 1999: 6), that is, commodities live social lives among the people who consume them.

During fieldwork in London, I spent a great deal of time in Malaysian halal restaurants, in butcher's shops, grocery stores, supermarkets, and hypermarkets selling halal products. Ritually slaughtered meat is the primary halal commodity, but a whole range of new commodities is now being subjected to halal requirements by Muslim organizations, groups, and consumers. So far, scholarly attention to halal in Britain has for the most part focused on conflicts over the provision of halal in schools (Abbas 2005), the politics of religious slaughter (Charlton and Kaye 1985; Kaye 1993; Bergeaud-Blackler 2004, 2007), and the marketing of halal meat (Ahmed 2008). In Ahmed's study of the marketing of halal meat in the United Kingdom between local shops and supermarkets, he concludes that "it is obvious that economic and marketing analysis alone will not provide a satisfactory solution to the type of consumer buyer behaviour...These issues and problems also have religious, traditional, ethical and industrial relations dimensions" (Ahmed 2008: 667). Despite the emergence of halal trade on a global scale, there have been no attempts to explore systematically the social, moral, and religious effects of what I call the proliferation of halal commodities.

The initial stage of the research in London was quantitative in method and outlook. Informants were selected on the basis of a survey that covered 100 mainly Malay respondents. The design of the survey primarily served to map migration trajectories, broader halal consumption patterns, and informants' understandings and practices of different types of halal certification in London.

On the basis of the survey, 14 Malay key informants were selected for interviewing (almost all interviews took place in Malaysian (halal) restaurants) and participant observation. During fieldwork, I also went shopping for halal with Malay consumers. More specifically, I explored the availability of halal products, including those certified by the Malaysian state.

Issues discussed included halal in science, business and religion, ethnicity and trust, food scares, meat, halal and wholesomeness, the politics of halal, and expanding halal requirements. Moreover, a number of background interviews and participant observations were carried out with halal producers and traders, Islamic organizations, and food authorities.

Extended periods of fieldwork in Kuala Lumpur and London have generated a variety of materials allowing me to explore the proliferation of halal from an anthropological perspective at different levels of the social scale: in the everyday lives of consumers and as a phenomenon inseparable from expanding markets, state certification, Islamic revivalism, and capitalist transformations.

To sum up, during fieldwork the following types of material were generated. First, participant observation was carried out among Muslim producers, entrepreneurs, traders, and consumers in restaurants, at halal exhibitions, and in shops in Kuala Lumpur and London. Thus, this book builds on multisited ethnography tracing the flows of people, goods, and ideas involved in halal. Second, in-depth interviews were conducted with Islamic organizations, food authorities, restaurant owners, halal entrepreneurs, *imams* (Muslim men who lead the prayers in a mosque), and Muslim consumers. Third, a survey in London designed to map halal provided me with valuable statistical information on the particularities of everyday halal understanding and practice. Fourth, I explored the proliferation of halal in media such as magazines, newspapers, e-mails, websites, advertisements, pamphlets, and menus in restaurants. Last, photographs taken by the author demonstrate that halal forms a part of Muslim space making in contemporary London.

I examine ways in which modern halal opens up for a range of questions that reinvigorates some old discussions within the anthropology of religion and food as well as the globalization of halal as a religious market in an era of mass consumption and marketing. The central focus is how middle-class Malay diasporic groups consume and negotiate halal in the interfaces between powerful Malaysian state discourses, the secular state, and Islamic organizations in Britain. An important issue is that religion and food are being linked and reconfigured in novel ways, and these transformations (e.g., related to spirituality, nutrition, distinctions, politics, identities, and globalization) call for renewed attention from the perspective of the anthropology of religion.

Organization of the Book

The book is organized around seven chapters. In Chapter 2, "Halal and Malay Middle-Class Mobility in Malaysia," I explore the emergence of the Malay middle-class in Malaysia in the interfaces between revivalist Islam, state, and market; the significance of halal and other forms of consumption among this class; and ethnicity and Malaysia's vision to become the world leader in halal. In other words, this chapter pinpoints how halal has become entangled in complex webs of political, ethnic, and national significance in modern Malaysia. Built on my previous periods of research on Islam and consumer culture among middle-class Malays in urban Malaysia, the main function of these discussions is to provide a broader context for exploring halal from a multisited perspective that follows middle-class Malays from Malaysia to Britain and traces the global circulation of halal commodities. Finally, I give an introduction to Malays currently living in Britain. I end this chapter with locating my diasporic Malay informants within the middle-class universes of Malaysia and Britain in terms of socioeconomic differentiation, that is, mapping these informants as representatives of the broad class terrain in a diasporic context.

Chapter 3, "Between Halal and the Secular in London," explores the emergence of London as a frontier for halal production, trade, and consumption. At the same time as this is happening, the meanings and practices of halal are being radically transformed and contested.

Paradoxically, in the eyes of many Muslims in Britain, this proliferation of halal calls attention to secular government's unwillingness or
incapacity to regulate halal as a religious market. Especially among
Malays, who compare this type of "secular food" to state-regulated
halal in Malaysia, this may be the case. In other words, the more
the culture of Islamic consumption asserts itself, the more the state's
incapacity to define what is legitimate halal, and thus, the unity of
Islam is felt. I show how halal evokes a range of sensibilities, attitudes,
assumptions, and behavior that may support or undermine "the secular" as an epistemic category in everyday life. I argue that modern
forms of halal consumption in London challenge and reconfigure
what are often considered separate secular realms of the state and politics, on the one hand, and the intimacy of religious life and expression, on the other. A central theme is claims for authority through
halal articulated by Islamic organizations in Britain in the interfaces
between expanding markets, the secular, and the rights and demands
of a growing group of Muslim consumers. The way in which halal is
becoming delocalized and the power and authority of the Malaysian
state evoked through halal in the diaspora is also explored.

Chapter 4, "The Other Side of the Logo," argues that the proliferation of halal in a multitude of commoditized forms is premised on
complex understandings and practices of certification. The title of this
chapter indicates a point that is subject to empirical substantiation.
Although more and more types of halal certification, and thus logos
on halal products, are appearing in the halal market in London, in the
eyes of many Muslim consumers, this marking tells them relatively
little about the actual or intrinsic halalness of the product. I study
everyday understandings and practices of logos and certification and
the way in which these are informing a whole range of issues, such as
migration trajectories, social stratification, Islamic self-understanding, and the involvement of the state and Islamic organizations.

Chapter 5, "Urban Halal Landscapes," is an exploration of the
spaces in which my Malay informants in London consume halal. This
chapter analyzes the proliferation of halal in London as an urban
form of space making. Although Muslim space making in general
has been explored in a growing body of literature, the spatial contexts of producing, displaying, selling, and shopping for halal have

received modest attention. The central argument in this chapter is that shopping for halal cannot be divorced from the context in which it is bought. Hence, the spatial context (atmosphere/feel/ambience) of food consumption as practice may be just as significant as the intrinsic qualities of the food and its ingredients. Halal is shaped not merely by religious self-understanding but also by much more mundane understandings and practices. This chapter ends with a comparison between eating halal out and eating halal in in the lives of my informants.

Chapter 6, "Halal Sanitized," deals with the sanitization of halal in the modern scientific world, that is, how Malays in London understand and practice halal as part of modern discourses of meat/stunning, health/nutrition, food scares, science, heating/cooling binaries, and excess, as well as kosher and vegetarian food. This exploration entails an analysis of expanding halal markets, with halal being transformed into a question and concern with genetically modified products, for example. The central focus in this chapter is Malays' interpretations of how these transformations influence their everyday practices of halal in the local context. This chapter ends with a discussion of the ethical underpinnings involved in modern forms of halal consumption and discourse. From being an Islamic injunction in the Koran, halal both evokes and is evoked by a whole range of discourses. In other words, this chapter captures how halal sits uneasily in and between a plethora of powerful scientific, religious, and political discourses that often overlap. Ultimately, these issues evoke broader questions of authority in modern societies and reveal how religion and science do or do not relate to each other.

The "Conclusion" ties the findings of the book together. In short, I conclude that among many middle-class Malays in London, the expanding halal market requires a constant and shifting engagement that is often moral in nature. Indeed, some Malays find this seemingly boundless expansion of halal and certification into ever more commodities excessive and unnecessary. On the other hand, Malays in London are aware that halal evokes a whole range of moral, political, or patriotic sentiments that are formative of individual, group, and national identities. Thus, even the most pragmatic Malays recognize that a whole range of powerful discourses and practices conditions and is conditioned by modern forms of halal. This conclusion is organized around five overarching themes, that is, the politics of the national, diasporic identity, and ethnicity; economics in relation to Islam and Malaysia's role in the global market for religious/ethnic commodities; science/modernity highlighting the role of Islam in contemporary, secular settings; authority, particularly linked to the power involved in halal certification embedded in contemporary Malaysian and Islamic institutional discourses and practices; and everyday strategies as a response to the above transformations. These factors are all entangled in modern halal, and they effect pluralization of consumer choices and everyday strategies among many Muslim consumers.

Chapter 2

Halal and Malay Middle-Class Mobility in Malaysia

In this chapter, I discuss the way in which Islam has been nationalized and halal has been standardized in Malaysia. This has taken place through Malaysia's bold halal vision. I will provide a glimpse into Malaysia International Halal Showcase (MIHAS), social and physical mobility among the Malay middle class, food and middle-class practice, the ethnic Chinese and Malay other, and middle-class Malays in London. These discussions provide the reader with a broader context for exploring "halal" using a multisited perspective that follows Malays from Malaysia to Britain and traces the global circulation of halal commodities. I show that halal has become entangled in complex webs of political, ethnic, and national significance in modern Malaysia. The concept of a "frontier" refers to different arguments presented in this chapter. Malaysia is a good example of a frontier where different class, religious, and ethnic cultures interpenetrate in a dynamic manner. As we shall see, in modern Malaysia, halal is no longer a question of a national or inner frontier but part of a vision to globalize halal markets on a frontier such as London.

My exploration of the Malay Muslim diaspora in London elaborates and continues a study of what I have called *Proper Islamic Consumption* in Malaysia (Fischer 2008a).[1] Building on anthropological fieldwork among suburban Malay middle-class families outside Kuala Lumpur in 2001–2002, I argued that the more cultures of consumption assert themselves, the more controversies over what Islam is, or ought to be, are intensifying. As new consumer practices emerge, they give rise to new discursive fields within which the meaning of Islam and Islamic practice are being debated. Exploring consumption practices in urban Malaysia, this study showed how diverse forms of Malay middle-class consumption (e.g., of food, clothing, and cars) are understood, practiced, and contested as a particular mode of modern Islamic practice. The book illustrates ways in which the issue of "proper Islamic consumption" for consumers, the marketplace, and the state in contemporary Malaysia evokes a whole range of contradictory Islamic visions, lifestyles, and debates articulating what Islam is or ought to be.

One key effect of these transformations is the deepening and widening concern for halal commodities among Malay Muslims that I call *halalization*. Halalization signifies a major preoccupation with the proliferation of the concept of halal in a multitude of commodified forms.

A Nationalized Islam

Of the Malaysian population of around 25 million in 2004, about 61 percent are indigenous Malays (virtually all Muslims) and tribal groups, also labeled *bumiputera* (literally, sons of the soil); 24 percent are Chinese; and 7 percent are Indians (http://www.indexmundi. com/malaysia/demographics_profile.html). Since Malaysia gained independence from Britain in 1957, Malays have constitutionally only been Malays if they are Muslims, speak the Malay language, and adhere to Malay culture/customs. Malaysia is not an Islamic state, but Islam is Malaysia's official religion and is professed by more than 50 percent of the population. In principle, Islam's "official" role was for ceremonial purposes and public occasions while the nation would remain a secular state (Nagata 1994: 67). At the time of independence, United Malays National Organisation (UMNO) played a major role in determining the constitutional position of Islam as "the religion of the country, a wording believed sufficient to convey the intended notion of a secular state" (Funston 2006: 54) in the eyes of more Islamically oriented groups. Economically, Malaysia has sustained rapid development within the past three decades during which the meaning of Islam has become evermore contested.

The rise of divergent *dakwah* (literally, invitation to salvation) groups in the wider resurgence of Islam in Malaysia challenged the secular foundation of the Malaysian state. *Dakwah* is both an ethnic and a political phenomenon, which has transformed Malaysia for both Muslims and non-Muslims. From the 1970s onward, Parti Islam SeMalaysia (PAS), the Islamic opposition party that still enjoys widespread popularity, together with *dakwah* groups, criticized the policies of the government led by UMNO for having "un-Islamic colonial traditions and secular practices which separated religion from political, social and economic issues" (Jomo and Cheek 1992: 85).

Angkatan Belia Islam Malaysia or the Islamic Youth Movement of Malaysia (ABIM) is the major *dakwah* group in Malaysia. The organization was formed in 1971 and has traditionally retained its strongest support among students in the campuses of the larger universities in Malaysia. ABIM is a "fairly 'this-worldly,' universalistic religious organization, transcending national and some ethnic boundaries at the level of its leadership" (Nagata 1984: 104). The central message of the organization is that Islam is a self-sufficient way of life that contains the answer to all human universal problems (Shamsul 1994: 104). The ritualistic aspects of the faith are not of vital importance, so it is acceptable for men to wear Western-style shirts and trousers. In comparison with earlier generations of revivalists, ABIM emphasizes a direct engagement, in line with the modernist tradition, with holy texts, bypassing the received wisdom of *ulama* (Ong 1995: 174).

My fieldwork in suburban Malaysia in 2001–2002 took place on a true frontier. From my fourteenth-floor condominium balcony in a middle-class suburb about 15 kilometers west of Malaysia's capital, Kuala Lumpur, I had two quite distinct views beneath me: to one side my fieldwork site and to the other side a view over the lush and "rural" greenery of Sungai Penchala. Sungai Penchala had the status of a Malay reserve, meaning that formally only Malays could buy land in this area. Sungai Penchala was also the home of the commune of Darul Arqam (the group has now dispersed and a highway runs through the area). This *dakwah* group was significantly different from ABIM in several respects.

Darul Arqam or the House of Arqam was an Islamic group whose believers sought to follow the behavior of the Prophet Muhammad in everyday life. Followers appeared to engage in an ascetic lifestyle and deny themselves Western luxuries such as furnishings, television, radio, and other amenities. Established in 1971, Arqam developed into a commune comprising about 40 houses on eight acres of land. The group set up its own *surau* (prayer house), medical clinic, school, and a number of workshops.

Arqam cultivated and marketed an Islamic vision of Malay independence and prosperity through the production of a wide range of halal food products. Ideally, this vision was to ensure the group full independence from any kind of non-Muslim control. Arqam successfully promoted this vision of communal self-sufficiency, and their halal goods were traded throughout peninsular Malaysia.

The Malaysian National Fatwa (opinion concerning Islamic law issued by an Islamic scholar) Council banned the organization in 1994 reasoning that the movement and its leader, Ustaz (religious teacher) Ashaari, believed in the imminent appearance of the Mahdi (or hidden *imam*, a Muslim man who leads the prayers in a mosque), a key idea in Shia belief. From the viewpoint of Malaysian Sunni orthodoxy, this notion implies unseen power and sectarian secrecy (Ackerman and Lee 1997: 49–51). In the everyday lingo of the state and press in Malaysia, this is labeled "deviationism," persistently staged as an outside other threatening the nation and the state's visions of modernity. Deviationism in Malaysia was evoked as the other of the pure and modern national Islam promoted by the state. At the same time, the state had effectively curbed Arqam as the vanguard of halalization. Hence, state-institutionalized regulation of halal had become a question of mass consumption, and there is no national frontier on which the state and competing groups overtly struggle over halal understanding and practice in contemporary Malaysia.

To preempt *dakwah* groups such as Darul Arqam and PAS, the state started to "nationalize" Islam (Fischer 2008a). In fact, today Malaysian Islam may be the most monolithic and most state regulated in the Muslim world (Bakar 2008: 82). Thus, the state's attempt at molding a modern form of Malayness is intimately linked to challenging Islamic discourses or *dakwah*, each with particular ideas and standards of how to combine consumption and Islamic practice. To preempt these confrontations, the state aggressively engages in a reconceptualization of consumption that envisions the amalgamation of Malay ethnicity, consumption practices, and Islam. This ongoing project, which started in the early 1970s, is intensifying in the context of economic growth and globalization.

The nationalization of Islam means the increased centrality of Islam as a national and ethnic signifier in Malaysia. The logic of this nationalization is to see Islam equated with Malayness being the naturalized core of the Malaysian nation. This nationalization of Islam has initiated a broader fascination with the proper and correct "Islamic way of life." For example, this Islamic way of life entails consuming specific halal goods, which are seen to have a beneficial impact on domains such as the family, community, and nation. Halal is both a result of the increase in revivalism and an instrument of that resurgence that leads to ever greater involvement with Islam helping to promote the movement that produced it. Hence, the nationalization of Islam subordinated the secular in Malaysia.

What is more, in the eyes of the Malaysian state, the reflowering of Islamic ritual life that followed in the wake of *dakwah* is seen as regressive and unwanted. Instead, as a consequence of its de-emphasis on Islamic ritual practices, the state tries to transform ritual to make it compatible with proper Islamic consumption, and halalization plays an important part in this process. More specifically, halalization among middle-class Malays in Malaysia works as a process of formalization and ritualization through repetition. Ritualization can constitute a way of acting that distinguishes and privileges practice against the quotidian, most often as sacred or profane. From halal requirements concerning food, these ideas have deepened and widened to cover a whole range of commodities and practices (Fischer 2008b).

This tension between the state dominated by UMNO and revivalist Islam runs through all of Malaysia's modern history. Another example of the way the state tries to preempt *dakwah* groups and PAS is state censorship in the written and electronic media. However, the Internet has escaped direct censorship so far (Fischer 2009a).

Ironically, Islamic revivalist critiques of "secularism" and the "secular state/government" in Malaysia have helped shape and reinforce not only a unique type of powerful UMNO-driven state nationalism in Malaysia but also a highly commercialized version of Islam in which halal plays a significant role. Although this type of state-driven nationalism can be said to be secular in nature, it feeds into and is in itself fed by a whole range of divergent Islamic discourses.

The growing centrality of Islam in Malaysian society is also reflected in the bureaucratization of Malay ethnicity (Ackerman and Lee 1997: 33), that is, an officially ethnically plural state in which Malays are a favored ethnicity. An example of an Islamic bureaucratic body set up by the state is Institut Kefahaman Islam Malaysia or the Institute for Islamic Understanding established in 1992. The priority of state organizations such as the Institute for Islamic Understanding is to guide Malays to correct and rightful Islamic practices in everyday life even as religious views are challenged by persistent secularists. In effect, this allies the bureaucratic state with Islam even while the ultimate step of calling Malaysia an "Islamic state" is avoided. Since independence, notions of the sacred in Malaysia have taken on more political meanings (Ackerman and Lee 1997: 134), and this is also reflected in the Malaysian state's standardization of halal.

Standardizing Halal

Interestingly, the state in Malaysia strategically employs halal as a material sign to overcome critiques of excessive secularism. In fact, halal is promoted as bridging the religious and the secular, as an example of the compatibility of the ethnicized state, modern Islam, business, and proper Islamic consumption. In a way, the Malaysian state's promotion of halal among Malays in Malaysia and on the global stage can be seen as a form of buycott (Fischer 2007) that encourages Muslim consumers to buy locally manufactured and state-certified halal products. This section discusses the standardization of halal in Malaysia with special reference to the Malaysian state that in itself acts as a halal-certifying authority. This fact is inseparable from Malaysia's vision to become the world leader in rapidly expanding halal markets on a global scale.

Over the past three decades, the Malaysian state has effectively certified, standardized, and bureaucratized halal production, trade, and consumption. I take Malaysian halal standards and standardization to mean several things. These points warrant a discussion of

the concepts of standard and standardization. Standards and standardization can refer to the design and qualities of products as well as proper conduct of companies (e.g., with regard to the production, preparation, handling, and storage of halal), states, organizations, and individuals. Standards and standardization can be seen to be instruments of control and forms of regulation attempting to generate elements of global order (Brunsson and Jacobsson 2000: 1). Unlike nonstate-certifying bodies in Britain, for example, the Malaysian state can impose sanctions on companies that do not live up to Malaysian standards.

What is more, standards can also refer to persons with certain qualifications, knowledge, or skills (Brunsson and Jacobsson 2000: 5). An example of this, as we shall see, is the idea expressed by several of my Malay informants that halal ideally should be produced and handled by Muslims. Hence, standards can generate and reinvigorate social norms and directives (Brunsson and Jacobsson 2000: 14). At the same time, the meanings of standards may evoke ideas of similarity and uniformity—the standardized is that which supposedly is similar and follows rules (Brunsson and Jacobsson 2000: 14). Such rules also "specify what is proper behaviour, and ideas of appropriateness thus become associated with standardization; the standard way of doing things is often understood not only as the most usual, but also the generally accepted, normal, and even best way" (Brunsson and Jacobsson 2000: 15).

In a broader perspective, I see halal in Malaysia and the vision to globalize it as a form of "standardization" (Scott 1998)—an attempt by the state to standardize production, trade, and consumption to achieve legibility and simplification. This process of standardization is apparent in state halal certification, but standardization is also market driven. The globalization of halal as a religious market expands in the interfaces between state certification and delocalized markets, that is, the penetration of halal as a localized Malaysian practice by capitalism.

As part of Malaysia's halal vision, Badawi (2006: 172) describes how Malaysia aspires to become a global halal hub, and to do so, the country has "established the standard MS 1500: 2004 as an international benchmark for the certification of halal products." This standard prescribes guidelines for production, preparation, handling, and storage of halal. In Malaysia, it is the state that certifies halal.

Malaysia is described as a model country in terms of complying with halal standards, and the country has strong halal activity in food processing and the export/import trade as reflected in its systematization and standardization of halal certification. Moreover, halal certificates for imports of meat, food, and kindred products are mandatory (Riaz and Chaudry 2004: 35). In response to the expansion of food service establishments and the opening of international restaurants in Malaysia from the 1970s onward, a thorough enactment of laws, diverse procedures, and guidelines was worked out:

> The passage of the Trade Description (use of expression 'halal') Order of 1975 made it an offense to falsely label food as halal, and the Trade Description Act (halal sign marking) of 1975 made it an offense to falsely claim the food to be halal on signs and other markings. (Riaz and Chaudry 2004: 54)

After coming to power in 1981, the charismatic and outspoken prime minister, Mahathir Mohamad, set off the wave of institutionalizing and regulating halal. Mahathir was in many ways the architect behind modern Malaysia, and the social engineering policies aimed at manufacturing a Malay middle class, as I shall discuss in detail below. Mahathir actively nationalized the proliferation of halal and concentrated its certification in the realm of the state where it has remained. In 2003, Mahathir resigned after 22 years as prime minister.

The Malaysian state in 1982 set up a committee to evaluate the certification of halal commodities under the Islamic Affairs Division (later the Islamic Development Department of Malaysia) in the Prime Minister's Department (Riaz and Chaudry 2004: 54). This committee was exclusively responsible for "instilling halal awareness amongst food producers, distributors, and importers." Another responsibility was mandatory halal certification of all imported meat. More specifically, the Islamic Affairs Division of the Prime Minister's Department and the Department of Veterinary Services should approve all meat plants exporting to Malaysia (Riaz and Chaudry 2004: 52). Consequently, a company that "wishes to use the official Malaysian halal logo, the processing facility in the country of origin has to be inspected and evaluated for halal certification by a team of two audi-tors from JAKIM" (Riaz and Chaudry 2004: 52–53).

Standards and standardization are also evident in the anthology *Food and Technological Progress: An Islamic Perspective* (Sallah and Sobrian 2006a), produced by a Malaysian publisher. It illustrates the powerful halal discourses in Malaysia. One contribution in the book argues that in the modern Muslim world, food scares and food secu-rity are inseparable from halal concerns. This contribution argues that in Muslim majority Malaysia, the halal/haram dichotomy is "being handled with great care by the relevant authority" (Sallah and Sobrian 2006b: x).

In another contribution, the former minister of agriculture in Malaysia envisions that Malaysia and Indonesia could become halal hubs to compete with US and European halal production (Norwawi 2006: 13). He contends that the certification of halal should not be limited to only food but should also extend to "sourcing, packag-ing, storing, distribution, retailing and product information. In this regard, Malaysia can play a major role through its world-renowned standardisation and certification agency, SIRIM Berhad"[2] (Norwawi 2006: 13–14).

In the anthology, the managing director of the Islamic Council of Australia and his co-author pose the following question:

> Thus, what are the demographic imperatives of this market and the potential of halal food trade? Most important is that there are approxi-mately 1.4 billion Muslims in the world who are consumers of *halal* food. As such, the *halal* food market is the largest market in the world. The important criteria of the *halal*-importing countries are as follows: (i) have one of the highest per-capita incomes in the world; (ii) have the fastest growing middle classes in the world; (iii) import a significant proportion of their food needs; and (iv) have the highest rates of popu-lation growth in the world. (Chawk and Ayan 2006: 76)

In this type of discourse, the middle class is seen to be particularly knowledgeable and fastidious about halal, and it is this notion I shall explore. At the same time, the authors critique nonstate halal certi-fiers in Western countries such as the International and Nutrition Food Council of America (IFANCA) and Islamic Coordinating Council of Australia. These bodies are accused of representing "static" and "rudimentary know-how and management capability" in the proliferating halal market over the past 15 years (Chawk and Ayann 2006: 79).

In Malaysia, the state certifies Nestlé's production. Imported products produced by Nestlé are certified by IFANCA. These certifying bodies are competitors in the global market for halal certification, and a company such as Nestlé is meticulous about selecting certification that is acceptable in particular regional, national, and local markets.

Halal has spurred new forms of space making in the form of halal zones or parks. An example of this is the vision to construct Malaysia International Halal Park, which is being promoted as the first International Halal Park offering a world-class global gateway for halal industries, trade, and services, according to the company behind the endeavor (www.myhalalhub.org). Malaysia International Halal Park is driven by a Malaysian vision to establish a halal supply chain between Malaysia's Port Klang Free Zone, which is a mix of an industrial park and a free-trade zone conveniently located close to Malaysia International Halal Park and the Port of Rotterdam, now a halal-certified zone that is trying to position itself as a halal gateway into the European Union.

In December 2007, the Malaysian government announced that it had signed a memorandum of understanding with National Investment Management Ltd. of China to facilitate the participation of the country through US$500 million in foreign investments in the development and promotion of Malaysia International Halal Park. To attract foreign companies and investment to Malaysia International Halal Park and to Malaysia, state bodies and authorities such as Halal Industry Development Corporation are refining their methods of inspection, control, and discipline in scientific production.

A recent study of halal food and nonfood products in the United Kingdom by MATRADE, Malaysia's national trade promotion agency, maps the potential of this market. Owing to EU regulations, Malaysia is not allowed to export meat products to the European Union. Hence, the Malaysian bid to enter the EU market targets halal products such as ready-made sauces (without meat contents), confectionery, nutrients, vitamins, minerals, toiletries, cosmetics, extracts, flavoring, emulsifiers, coloring, fats, edible oils, and lipids for foods and the pharmaceutical industries as well as E467, E471, E472a, E472e, E481, and E482. The study states that "Malaysia's international image is that of a modern, progressive Muslim nation" and that the Malaysian halal logo and certification system is recognized in the United Kingdom as no single body in this market officially acts as a halal certifier (http://edms.matrade.gov.my/domdoc/Reports.nsf /svReport/86763F1A9777C47A482571010012E74B/$File/PMS -%20Halal_1.doc?OpenElement).

At the same time, 9/11 transformed Islam into both an agent and a product of globalization, making Islam a global phenomenon that demands an opinion about itself (Devji 2005). What is more, "Islam has come to occupy the language of faith globally" (Devji 2008: 191). As a sign of this, the article "The Halal Way to Free Trade" in *New Straits Times* (May 11, 2006), one of the most popular national papers in English in Malaysia, and published in connection with MIHAS, asserted that

> In the years since Sept 11 terror attacks, the halal market has grown from a tributary concern of the devout to the mainstream of the multitudes. Politics has combined with demographics to manufacture an economic demand of global proportions while supply, still highly localised and inward looking, struggles to catch up.

9/11 had become a global concern reconfiguring domestic politics in Malaysia and consolidated the country's position as a moderate Islamic state (Shamsul 2001: 7). Hence, post-9/11, the powerful state and corporate halal discourse in Malaysia identified this "moderate" Muslim country as a key player in the proliferation of global halal. The food scandal in Indonesia that was discussed in Chapter 1 seemed to reinforce Southeast Asian fastidiousness in this expanding market. Interestingly, the concern over halal is more pronounced in some Southeast Asian countries such as Malaysia, Indonesia, Brunei, and Singapore than in much of the Middle East and South Asia. The reasons for this are many, but the proliferation of halal in a country such as Malaysia cannot be divorced from the fact that the country over the past three decades has witnessed steady economic growth, the emergence of large groups of Malay Muslim middle-class consumers as well as centralized state incentives to strengthen halal production, trade, and consumption. Europe, the United States, Canada, and Australia, which have many South and Southeast Asian diasporas, are emerging as centers with large and growing Muslim populations and as major markets for halal.

Ironically, the demonization of Islam and Muslims that followed in the wake of 9/11 was complemented by the recognition that Muslims were also consumers with certain demands that were open to commercialization. It is in this context my ethnography from London should be seen, that is, the emergence of modern halal in the new millennium has become part of a globalized religious market. The Malaysian state is in itself a certifier of halal, and this is central to the processes of standardization that have taken place since the early 1980s. Consequently, Malaysia's bid to become the world leader in rapidly expanding halal markets on a global scale is entangled in complex webs of national and political significance.

"Networking, Consolidating and Energising": MIHAS 2006

I will now discuss my participant observation at MIHAS, in Kuala Lumpur that can be said to be the embodiment of halalization on a global scale. Indeed, Prime Minister Badawi's halal vision at MIHAS was a bold one: it reflected the desires of Badawi, who took office after Mahathir Mohamad in 2003, to promote halal as part of a state vision represented by UMNO; to proliferate halal globally as a healthy, pure, ethical, religious, and modern alternative in an era of food scares; the strategic targeting of the United Kingdom, Malaysia's former colonizer, and the European market—home to a large, expanding, and relatively wealthy Muslim population; Malaysia as a country where halal has become a legitimate taste or model standardized by the state; halal benefits for the *ummah* reconceptualized as ethical Muslim producers, traders, and consumers; and the revival of the golden past of Islamic trade networks.

Since its start in 2004, MIHAS has developed into an annual event. 2006 saw halal expos in Los Angeles, Jakarta, Paris, Brunei, Dubai, and Melbourne, among other places. In the eyes of the Malaysian state, halal producers and traders, and a plethora of Islamic organizations, the increase in such "network events" indicates the emergence

of a global halal "network" or community. MIHAS 2006, "themed" as "Networking, Consolidating and Energising," was held at the massive Malaysian International Exhibition & Convention Centre outside Kuala Lumpur.

At MIHAS 2004, Badawi proudly announced, "Today we will mark the unveiling of a new standard for Malaysia—a Muslim standard for the world." The prime minister was referring to the launch by the Malaysian Institute of Industrial Research and Standards (SIRIM) of a Malaysian Standard MS 1500, General Guidelines on the Production, Preparation, Handling and Storage of Halal Foods. Ideally, this new standard (prescribing guidelines for halal production, preparation, handling, and storage) should further strengthen Malaysian state halal certification in its efforts to cooperate with multinational companies.

MIHAS consisted of three main activities. First, seminars held by companies such as Tesco, the largest British retailer by both global sales and domestic market share, and Malaysian state organizations, for example, MATRADE and Jabatan Kemajuan Islam Malaysia or the Islamic Development Department of Malaysia (JAKIM). Participation in these seminars provided me with an insight into the halal vision in the interfaces or gray zones between the state, business, and religious revivalism. It struck me that this was the first time I witnessed such a determined, smooth, and direct commercialization of halal and Islam in Malaysia. Time and again, reference was made to the state's halal logo as a pure and trustworthy "gold standard" state certification or brand to be exported in an era of food scares and mistrust. In a booklet that was handed out at MIHAS, the Minister of International Trade and Industry argued that "the Malaysian *halal* logo exemplifies the nation's commitment to the adherence of religious tenets as well as the internationally recognized health and safety standards" (MATRADE 2006: iii).

We learned that Malaysia should be alert to competition from skilled networking nations such as Brunei, Singapore, Thailand, and Indonesia. Consequently, the government has established 32 offices worldwide, an "overseas network," including an office in London.

Second, this halal trade fair included "trade-matching programs" and "networking sessions" in which producers, traders, and buyers could come together. The day before MIHAS started, Badawi declared that the halal market can be used to rally Muslims (*The Star*, May 11, 2006), and that governments and companies should use MIHAS to help establish Malaysia as a halal hub. During this event, the deputy minister for Entrepreneurial and Cooperative Development was quoted as stating that Malay entrepreneurs at MIHAS especially should "grab this opportunity to enhance their business networking at the international level" (*New Straits Times*, May 13, 2006). After MIHAS, another article (*The Star*, May 18, 2006) concluded that this halal event was a "huge success," and that it had proved to be "the most cost effective platform for halal world players to promote their products, as well as to widen their business networking and trade activities globally." The *New Straits Times* on May 18, 2006, wrote that "Halal Showcase Rakes in Deals Worth RM168m."

Third, MIHAS included a large number of product demonstrations and samples. These product demonstrations testified to the fact that, in Malaysia, halal has also proliferated into a wide range of nonfood products (toiletries, medication, and health products) and services such as banking, insurance, and education. The global trend in recent years has been to see that a thriving business in Islamic goods has emerged. Everything from stickers, rugs, holiday cards, and plaques with Islamic calligraphy to special types of holidays aimed at Muslim audiences, watches displaying *salat* (prayer times) and other features, logos and ring tones on mobile phones, clothes, and so on touch upon and "Islamicize" virtually every aspect of life (D'Alisera 2001: 97). At the same time, there has been a marked change from craft production to mass production of religious commodities (Starrett 1995).

As one would expect, MIHAS was an essential arena for the performance of halal networking, in particular with respect to exchanging business cards, and I was soon to receive e-mails advertising new products and announcing new halal trade fairs around the world.

Among the entrepreneurs I met at MIHAS was a Malay woman, Jeti, who in many respects reflects the ways in which networking is involved in Malaysian halal. She holds degrees in accounting and business studies from the United Kingdom and is currently involved in promoting halal for the Malaysian state by organizing trade promotions. She also has a private company. She acknowledges that to develop halal, consumer needs must be mapped out in detail. Therefore, Jeti recognizes the necessity of participating in events such as MIHAS to establish an international network of people working in the fields of halal research and business. Of particular interest to Jeti is the promising U.K. market, which she knows from her studies there and which figures so prominently in the Malaysian state's halal vision. I also had the opportunity to meet Jeti later that year at the Halal Exhibition at the World Food Market (WFM) held in London in November 2006, which had developed into a significant network event in which a MATRADE delegation also participated.

At the Halal Exhibition, Jeti envisaged halal as giving Malaysia an edge and a "niche trade network," whereas Europe and the United States otherwise dominate global trade. The news that Nestlé had entered into a halal business deal with Malaysia was proof to Jeti that it is only in cooperating with multinationals and using their existing trade networks that a country such as Malaysia can succeed.

Jeti is confident that the emerging halal trade is forging new Malay "community networks" on a global scale. Unlike the Chinese and the Indians, Malays were traditionally "confined" to Malaysia. Now there is the political will to promote Malaysia in terms of halal internationally, and this is indicative of a major shift toward a more global attitude.

In his opening speech at MIHAS 2006, Badawi stated that this year MIHAS had "cast the net wider" with the inclusion of seminars and talks by a long list of countries and companies. New imagined trade networks always involve some form of location and are thus both political and moral constructions of space and place, so that networks cannot be free from the ties that imagined them (Green, Harvey, and Knox 2005: 807). MIHAS had become a global network event that celebrated Malaysian political business, nationalism, and modern forms of Islamic consumer culture. The question is how Malays generally understood and practiced this proliferation of halal in everyday life in London. In other words, I shall in detail discuss to what extent the state and corporate discourses on halal and diaspora filter down to be understood, practiced, or contested.

The Ethnic and Malay Other

This section explores two significant others in powerful discourses on halal in Malaysia—ethnic Chinese and what Michael Peletz (1997: 231) has called "ordinary Malays," that is, Malays who are not in the forefront of contemporary religious or political developments and who are somewhat ambivalent about these.

In contemporary Malaysia, even many Chinese shops and restaurants have started putting up signs and selling state-certified products, and they are thus recognized as "halalized." In other words, these Chinese shops are now subjected to state-controlled halalization. This section does not purport to be a systematic exploration of halal among the substantial Chinese minority community in Malaysia. Instead, I explore how the Malaysian state's interpretation of halal is quite often directed against this group.

The powerful halal discourses in Malaysia are discussed in the book *Halal Haram: A Guide by Consumers Association of Penang* (2006) published by a local Malaysian consumers' association that has status as a nongovernmental organization (NGO). In many ways, this book addresses the questions I shall explore in the following chapters. First, it argues for an intimate relationship between spirituality and Islam: "The saying 'You are what you eat' is well-recognised in Islam....the cleanliness of the body literally depends on the food we consume" (Consumers Association of Penang 2006: 12). Moreover, "from the spiritual aspect...a Muslim has to keep himself pure by consuming only clean food because Allah is pure and loves [the] purity of men" (Consumers Association of Penang 2006: 12). Second, based on production context, handling, and ethnicity, the book contends that food deriving from animals reared under cruel conditions is haram (Consumers Association of Penang 2006: 14). Factors that determine halal status are "the nature of the foodstuff itself, how it is produced, processed, distributed and how it is acquired" (Consumers Association of Penang 2006: 16). What is more, Muslims must "realise that the kitchen, crockery and cooking utensils must also be free from *Haram* substances before the food served can be considered *Halal*" (Consumers Association of Penang 2006: 38). Third, and most important in this context, the book states that "Malaysia is a multiracial country with various ethnic groups and religions. In view of this, the issue of Halal/Haram is of great importance, as many non-Muslims do not understand the Islamic dietary rules" (Consumers Association of Penang 2006: 19). This point is especially pertinent to Malay Muslims in a non-Muslim diasporic context on a frontier such as London.

In Malaysia, ethnic distinctions are often expressed through food. In the eyes of rural Malay fishermen, Thai and Chinese are quintessential pork eaters regardless of actual dietary practice. Thus, these ethnic groups are expressive of ritual contamination that can only be negated by conversion to Islam (Firth 1966).

Unsurprisingly, in the eyes of some Malays, the Chinese may be omnivorous, whereas Malays, in line with halalization, are particular and sensitive about food. Logically, the halalized food domain must be protected from the "pollution of indifference." In a wider perspective, these ideas fit an analysis of the everyday conceptualization of fixed and uncontested Chinese economic success (Yao 2002: 3–4). Thus, the hardworking, economically successful Chinese come "alive in the twilight zone between reality, ideological construction and social imagination" (Yao 2002: 4). It will be clear how the relevance of these ethnic relations conditions Malay understandings and practices of halal in London.

It is a generally held idea among many Malays that the Chinese are skilled and cunning networkers. Once these business or social networks of Chinese entrepreneurs have been conceptualized, such networks become real and only bear benefits for those inside them (Yao 2002: 143). As part of the state discourse on halal, Malays have a moral obligation to support Muslim businesses, as the Chinese have always supported their own ethnic group through complex networks of loyalty, questionable moral business standards, and a concealed system of credit given only to Chinese. In Malay national myths, Chinese material enjoyment is often fueled by doubts about Chinese possession of national devotion because of more powerful ethnic loyalties. Rather, the Chinese are seen to possess an "ethnic surplus." In Malaysia, class distinctions between Malays and Chinese in particular often materialize in the gray zones between religion, ethnicity, the state, and modes of consumption.

Halal in Malaysia is also to a large extent directed against the "bad Malay other" and often this persona is coded generationally. This "bad

Malay" can represent the diversity of halal practice in rural Malaysia and traces of a history in which halal was quite situational, contingent, and personal. This, in turn, can be seen just as much as a "dangerous" other to the Malaysian state and Islamic revivalist discourses as the Chinese. In fact, halal in Malaysia quite often targets the older generation of Malays. As we shall see, what Malays in London currently do resembles what Malays until the 1980s did in Malaysia. Prior to the wave of Islamic revivalism in Malaysia, Malays practiced forms of halal that allowed them some degree of flexibility to participate in the lives of their non-Muslim friends and neighbors. For example, it was not unusual for Malays to attend the gatherings and celebrations of their Chinese and Indian neighbors, despite the fact that "haram" elements may be present in such gatherings. The ability to balance one's own notions of piety with the practices, customs, and desires of non-Muslim neighbors was an essential aspect of living for Malays of previous generations. The widespread notion among Indian, Chinese, and Malay communities that one essential, substantive aspect to belonging is eating together, that is, the sharing of substance, was crucial to sociality in past times and is now critical in more contemporary imaginations of "essential" difference today. For previous generations, eating together required tact, care, and vigilance on all sides but largely did not compromise one's sense of proper living.

As we shall see, Malays in London largely manage to negotiate religious diversity, as it contingently arises by doing something that their parents and grandparents used to do in Malaysia itself. At the same time, halal in Malaysia today largely prevents such interactions, and the powerful state discourses on halal play an important part in this process. Consequently, not only do contemporary understandings of halal tend to position Malays against the Chinese other, the state version of halal also often positions the younger Malays against their Malay parents and grandparents in terms of how halal and piety should be practiced in everyday life. The main point here is that the acceptance of halal among diverse socioeconomic groups of Malays in Malaysia is not universal. I have suggested (Fischer 2008a) that making distinctions between two Malay groups in Malaysia is a highly uneven process full of ambiguities and contradictions. What is appearing, then, are two Malay registers of modern lifestyles. First, one group performs proper Islamic consumption as a localized form of purism, for example, younger groups of pious Malays that tend to be fastidious about halal. Second, another group of middle-class Malays ("ordinary Malays") is more oriented toward a pragmatic approach to halal understandings and practices. The more puristic or fastidious some Malay individuals or groups may be about halal in Malaysia, the more the ethnic Chinese other can be seen as problematic.

The Making of the Malay Middle Class

In the 1970s, the Malaysian state launched the New Economic Policy (NEP) to improve the economic and social situation of the Malays vis-à-vis the Chinese in particular. The NEP entailed a number of benefits for the Malays and other indigenous groups, such as increased ownership of production and preferential quotas in the educational system. The number and proportion of Malays engaged in the modern sector of the economy rose significantly as a result of these policies. Ideologically, the overall objective was to produce an educated, entrepreneurial, shareholding, high-consuming, and socially/physically mobile Malay middle class, which the state elite views as a necessary prerequisite for economic, national, and social cohesion. Mahathir became the proponent of this policy. This piece of grand social engineering is essential to understand the middle-class terrain of Malaysia and the social and physical mobility of these Malays.

At the same time, the NEP of the Malaysian state has forged a new class of Malay entrepreneurs, *Melayu Baru* or New Malays. According to Mahathir Mohamad (1995: 1), the New Malay embodies an aggressive, entrepreneurial, and global "we can" mentality. In 1991, Mahathir unveiled Vision 2020, which pictured Malaysia as a fully developed nation by the year 2020, and this New Malay mentality is seen as essential for achieving this goal. The coining of this term by Mahathir signifies the concretion of a hardworking and entrepreneurial urban Malay middle-class mentality. In effect, the novel Islamic ethos in Malaysia is tied to allegiance to the state evoked as a form of cultural kinship through religion (Ong 1999: 226). My Malay middle-class informants in London can be seen to belong to this group of New Malays.

As a consequence of the growing middle class in Malaysia, consumption has been subjected to state and business intervention in the form of extensive market research and the political institutionalization of consumption, an example of this was the setting up of the Ministry of Domestic Trade and Consumer Affairs in 1990. Clearly, this is a sign of the state's bid to become an apparently "honest broker" of consumption (Zukin 2004) that protects the entitlements of Malaysian consumers against what the state and consumers increasingly see as confusing and excessive consumer culture. What is more, since the 1980s, shopping spaces have been "standardized," that is, supermarkets and hypermarkets have become favorite outlets among middle-class groups.

There seems to be a paradoxical blurredness and imprecision of the middle-class concept, on the one hand, and, on the other, its ability to explain the origins of the modern world (Wallerstein 1991: 143). Hence, the middle class occupies a mythical place in the advent of development and modernity—the emergence of this class "expanded the realm of monetary transaction and unleashed thereby the wonders of the modern world" (Wallerstein 1991: 143). The explanatory validity and value of this myth may be limited. It is, nevertheless, obvious that for a developing economy such as Malaysia, the emergent middle class and New Malays have become an almost mythical national signifier of mental and material development. This myth is very much alive and has been internalized as a significant point of self-understanding among the Malaysian middle class and political elites. The state elite views the creation of such a class as a necessary prerequisite for economic, national, and social cohesion (Embong 1998: 85).

Middle-Class Malays as an Aesthetic Community

When asked about self-definition in terms of class during my 2001–2002 fieldwork in suburban Malaysia, all informants without exception, but for different reasons, referred to themselves as *kelas pertengahan* (middle class). To informants, the term "middle" appeared to be a convenient way of signifying social mobility attained through education, occupation, and family background. Although the state may be a major ideological driving force behind the manufacturing of a Malay middle class, the force of the market and capitalist relations of production should not be downplayed (Embong 1998: 86). My study showed that Malays usually had a tertiary education, often worked as professionals, and earned a relatively high income.

I have shown that class should be treated as an emic and performative category and explored how objective parameters of class (education/occupation/income) were involved in class practices or performances, that is, particular kinds of reflexive and strategic practices. The iterability of performances is highly formative of social relationships such as class (Goffman 1971: 27).

Debates over proper modes of Malay halal consumption are of particular significance among the Malay middle class, as it is within this intermediate group that the nature of what Islam is or ought to be is most strongly contested.

The nature of the middle-class suburb in which my ethnography took place was "deep," that is, intimately private: one- and two-story terraced and semidetached houses, bungalows, and condominiums are all constructed as fortified enclaves whose primary function is to house middle-class families. A suburb like this is planned to be clean, constructed around family values, and focused on recreational facilities such as parks and playgrounds. This type of modern and affluent suburb monumentally symbolizes the progress of the Malaysian nation in a postcolonial context, the celebration of the growth of the middle class, and the ordering of space into manageable and exploitable form. Such a Malaysian middle-class suburb enjoys the convenience of modern local mosques and shopping facilities, and, eventually, has come to experience the tension that arises between Islam and what is seen as excessive consumption in this local context. Most of this shopping is done in malls, and moral panic in connection with (*lepak*) loitering by teenagers is deeply felt among many families. In fact, many middle-class residents consider the city of Kuala Lumpur immoral and threatening, that is, the city signifies crime and pollution.

Any object in this suburban middle-class setting could be perceived as excessive or improperly handled or displayed. With regard to housing (size of the house/interior decoration), cars (foreign luxury cars versus smaller and Malaysian-produced Proton cars), and dress (displaying class through the wearing of designer brands while piously covering the body), for example, the Malay middle class is split between individual consumer desires in the market for identities (Navaro-Yashin 2002), on the one hand, and heartfelt social anxieties about the moral and social integrity of the families, on the other. In this multitude of everyday decisions and debates, there is a marked tension between notions of "excess" and "balance." Understandings of proper Islamic consumption are determined by constant attempts to resolve this tension. Unsurprisingly, the social and physical mobility of the suburban Malay middle class has improved drastically compared with previous generations.

With the extension of consumer goods markets and their advertising in Malaysia from the late 1970s, a complex ideology or social ontology of consumption was required (Mazzarella 2003: 12). The emergence of such a new ontology of consumption was felt most forcefully in the advertising of images that reflected the desire of individual consumers and simultaneously presented "a generalized sounding board for the national community, now reconceptualized as an aesthetic community" (Mazzarella 2003: 13). This type of aesthetic community with its own social ontology of consumption is distinguished by its taste preferences, which are most clearly pronounced in the emerging middle class—being a social person or possessing a certain identity through sets of proper Malay Muslim consumption.

New forms of Malay aesthetic communities have emerged out of halalization based on different taste preferences in various middle-class fractions. This proliferation of halalization has stimulated a range of elaborate ideas about the boundaries and authenticity of halal purity versus haram impurity. The idea of Malays as a particular aesthetic community emerging in the interfaces between state social engineering, Islamic revivalism, and the marketplace also applies to Malays as a diasporic community on the frontier. The aesthetic community is intertwined with the moral community, so that "ideas about purity and pollution, good and evil articulate the two and . . . may generate moral conflicts about the legitimacy of aesthetic forms, or, indeed, of a morality which rejects these valorised forms" (Werbner 1996: 92). My point is that halal always intertwines the aesthetic and the moral simultaneously.

The aesthetic can also be seen as a mode of apprehending reality or as a mode of articulating/constituting the real (Viladesau 1999: 8). Theological aesthetics considers religion in relation to sensible knowledge, that is, sensation, imagination, and feeling (Viladesau 1999: 11). I think halal is a good example of the interplay between aesthetics and the more mundane in the form of shopping that is also informed by convenience, thrift, and health, for example. These points will be explored on the basis of halal understanding and practice in the lives of my informants.

In William James's seminal work *Varieties of Religious Experience. A Study in Human Nature* (2002), he argues that the "æsthetic motive" is endemic to religion (James 2002: 355). It is central to James's (2002: 375) conceptualization of religion that "the visible world is part of a more spiritual universe from which it draws its chief significance." For Muslims, halal is simultaneously a manifestation of the visible and mundane world of shopping, on the one hand, and a spiritual universe, on the other hand—food is employed simultaneously in both symbolic systems and ritual ceremonies and everyday choice (Korsmeyer 1999: 4). I will show that halal helps shape both a moral and an aesthetic community among the Malays in London. In other words, halal is inseparable from individual and group trajectories. My ethnographic and multisited approaches to these trajectories constitute a historical context for the exploration of halal as globalized religious market on the frontier.

Malay Middle-Class Food

Malaysian middle-class taste in food, the context of buying it, and the transformation of the kitchen where it is being prepared are now the center of attention. Statistically and through interviewing and participant observation in my suburban fieldwork site, it was evident that house culture among middle-class Malays is being transformed because the kitchen in the typical Malay middle-class house has been radically modernized and industrialized with the import of a multitude of kitchen appliances. At the same time, the urban landscape of (food) consumption in and around Kuala Lumpur has changed drastically since the 1980s. Economic growth, the emergence of a large middle class, and globalization of the food market have pluralized everyday shopping choices.

Food consumption holds a special position in Bourdieu's seminal work *Distinction: A Social Critique of the Judgement of Taste* (1984). For Bourdieu (1984: 2), consumption including that of food works as "communication, that is, an act of deciphering, decoding, which presupposes practical or explicit mastery of a cipher or code." This culture of knowledge and practice works as a "principle of pertinence" enabling consumers "to identify, among the elements offered to the gaze, all the distinctive features and only these, by referring them, consciously or unconsciously, to the universe of possible alternatives" (Bourdieu 1984: 4). Distinction can refer to difference or recognition of difference between, first, objects or people or, second, excellence in quality, talent, honor, or respect (Bourdieu 1984). Social identity, particularly in respect to class, Bourdieu (1984: 172) maintains, is defined, asserted, and practiced through difference. More specifically, middle-class knowledge of manners or styles as symbolic manifestations constitutes one of the key markers of middle-class identity and is an ideal weapon in distinctions (Bourdieu 1984: 66). The concern for the symbolic, appearance, pretension, and bluff are all genuine marks of the middle class (Bourdieu 1984: 253).

Before entering into a discussion about food consumption practices, I outline some more general points about food culture in Malaysia. Chinese, Indian, Thai, Western, and many other influences have shaped the Malaysian national cuisine. *Rempah*, a spice paste, is central to many Malay dishes, and this is also the case with *belancan* (shrimp paste or sauce). As could be expected, rice plays an important role in Malaysia in the culinary traditions of Malays, Indians, and Chinese. Festive occasions call for dishes such as *nasi himpit* (compressed rice cubes), *rendang daging* (rich coconut beef), and *sayur lodeh* (curried vegetable stew). Other popular dishes are *satay* (pieces of diced or sliced meat, fish, or tofu that are grilled and served with various spicy seasonings including peanut sauce), varieties of *nasi goreng* (fried rice), *mee goreng* (fried noodles), *ayam percik* (grilled chicken dipped in rich coconut gravy and spices), and *nasi lemak* (rice cooked in coconut milk served with a spicy pasta, boiled eggs, and anchovies).

Malaysian Indian food includes banana leaf rice (white rice served on a banana leaf with an assortment of vegetables, curry meat or fish, and *papadum*, which is a crispy flatbread), *biryani* (a mixture of spices, basmati rice, meat/vegetables, and yogurt), curries, and *roti canai* (a thin bread that is fried and served with condiments). Indian Muslims, Mamak, developed a particular and popular cuisine in Malaysia that includes *nasi kandar* (rice served with other dishes of curry with chicken, fish, beef, or mutton and often together with vegetables) and *mee mamak* (fried eggs and noodles).

Basically, Malaysian Chinese food is inspired by mainland Chinese cuisine, but it has been blended with local food cultures. Many Chinese dishes involve pork as a subingredient. Often these dishes are also available in versions with chicken to accommodate Muslim tastes. An example of a popular Chinese dish in Malaysia is *bak kut the* (pork ribs soup). Malays enjoy many other Chinese dishes such as *nasi ayam hailam* (chicken rice) as long as they are seen to be properly subjected to halal requirements.

Nyonya food, a mix of Chinese and Malay cuisines, is the food of the Peranakan people of Malaysia and Singapore, descendants of Chinese immigrants who to a large extent have adopted local Malay culture. Nyonya food is one aspect of the millennia-old and diverse interaction between East and Southeast Asia (Anderson 2007). Typical dishes are *asam laksa* (rice noodles served in a fish, vegetables, and spices) and *laksa lemak* (laksa served in a rich coconut gravy). In sum, the Malaysian national cuisine is heavily influenced by the country's multiethnic composition.

However, the proliferation of halal has reconfigured these culinary exchanges. This does not mean that Malays typically will only eat traditional Malay dishes, but that the dishes of the other are subjected to novel forms of halal requirements. On top of these types of ethnic or "national" foods, a wide range of mainly Western and Asian restaurants and fast food outlets are prominent in urban Malaysia. Unproblematically, my informants would frequent local Malay restaurants, *mamak* food stalls serving Indian Malaysian food, as well as Kentucky Fried Chicken and McDonald's, as these were fully halal certified. All of this testifies to a form of Malaysianized cosmopolitanism that is characteristic of these middle-class Malays.

In my study among middle-class Malays, I learned that besides a refrigerator and oven, the vast majority of families, regardless of class grouping, owned a toaster, blender/mixer, microwave oven, baking machine, rice cooker, juice maker, electric kettle, and a number of other appliances. These transformations of the inner domain of the middle class mirror wider societal changes, most notably in the form of increased affluence, material status, and the fact that a large number of Malay middle-class women worked outside the home while still being in charge of buying groceries and preparing food.

Food consumption and its religious, social, and cultural context may be the closest one can come to a core symbol in the everyday lives of Malay families. I was invited to celebrations in the homes of informants on numerous occasions. A typical dish served in these homes was beef cooked in rich coconut gravy (*rendang daging*), a dish that is often on the menu at home and in Malaysian restaurants in London.

My empirical material showed that middle-class Malays as their first priority bought groceries from a supermarket in a nearby mall followed by a wet market, a minimarket, a hypermarket, and finally from a local grocery store. Typically, respondents and informants would go to several different shops to buy groceries. Consequently, the vast number of choices with respect to buying groceries indicates that strategies involved in food consumption have increased in the wake of the pluralization of the food market.

The study indicated that the halal/haram dichotomy is not only about maintaining the separateness of these two binaries but simultaneously also about protecting the status of the sacred against the impurity of the profane. An example of this could be the separation of halal and haram food products in supermarkets. The nonhalal products are for the most part stored in a small, secluded room away from the main shopping area. Hence, sacred or profane effects are to a large extent generated in objects by inscription, classification, and context. Of course, the way in which these effects are presented is of crucial importance. The same tendency is visible with regard to restaurants that are also marked and certified as either halal (all Kentucky Fried Chicken and McDonald's outlets in Malaysia are fully halal certified) or nonhalal (e.g., a number of Chinese restaurants).

Furthermore, the mass availability of imported food increases anxieties about contamination, while this food may also be a sign of refined and exotic taste. This is symptomatic of and corresponds to the commercialization of the kitchen within each Malay middle-class home as described above. In short, food consumption is a crucial component in the market for middle-class identities.

Two different types of approaches to the field of proper Malay food consumption emerged. First, some of these middle-class Malays preferred food that was simple, appetizing, and economical. Necessity is the driving logic in this type of reasoning, signified by price consciousness and thrift.

The second approach is extreme variation, that is, going to every kind of shop for various reasons. In this instance, the buying of food appears to be a highly ritualized practice that involves careful planning and organization. Its ritualistic features emerge as reiterated and temporally structuring practices that require certain skills and knowledge for optimal performance, for example, being conscious of the particular audience or guests in the middle-class home. One of my informants, an affluent woman in her 50s, declared that she would serve almost anything depending on the particular audience of her performances. If there were "special" guests such as foreigners she would serve something "ethnic." This clear example of performance signifies how food works to constitute class as a performative category through proper knowledge of legitimate taste. Among Malay middle-class families sharing food and socializing with the other ethnic groups was, at best, limited to yearly open house arrangements. This informant preferred to serve Chinese and Indians "national food," for example, *rendang daging* or *nasi lemak*, as if to compensate for their lack of nationness and reembodiment of the national. In this instance, the performance aspect depends on the proper audience and its ability to recognize legitimate taste in a globalized food market.

Another informant, a man in his 40s, who was involved in *dak-wah* work and owned an IT company, particularly embodied the power of halalization involved in consumer preferences in everyday life. He minutely divided Malays into segments according to their adherence to extremely elaborate ideas about what was considered Islamically acceptable and what was not. These distinctions produced and maintained purity versus impurity and, in the end, legitimate Islamic taste. There was an expression of halalization as the support of Malays vis-à-vis the Chinese through consumption. Consequently, he maintained that his favorite shops were smaller Malay-owned ones to support Muslim businesses. These more puristically oriented Malays work hard to stretch food halalization to involve proper preferences, taste, handling, presentation, and context. Thus, the whole complex of food has been subjected to processes of ritualization in a world of consumer choices.

The uncertainty involved in food consumption seems to incite this new form of stringency within the logics of halalization. The halalness of a product is not directly verifiable through smell or appearance, so, as in the case of organic products, it is mainly a question of trust in its certification. Ideally, this certification will remove or mend malevolence in the commodity.

Everyday choices based on convenience and thrift often seemed to be the determinant factors for my informants' decisions. Informants reflected a general adherence to halal principles in terms of food. All informants conveyed that this was the single most significant principle. What is more, marketing research shows that Malays react more positively to advertisements with halal signage than they do to those without (Hassan et al. 2009: 258). Food has traditionally been subject to the inscription of Islamic understandings of halal and haram, and from this starting point, these ideas have deepened and widened in Malaysia to be inscribed into a large number of other object domains. Historically, the halal/haram distinctions in Malaysia gained momentum in the wake of *dakwah* but have been diversified and individualized as understanding and practice in everyday life.

Capitalism is adjusting to the recent requirements of a growing number of Muslims in Malaysia, and the Islamic market is expanding rapidly. Informants explained that previously it was very difficult to go to a restaurant and ask if products were halal or not because there were no "signs" or "logos." In the end, it is the privilege of the state to recognize and standardize these businesses according to halal requirements, which obviously is an immensely complex endeavor inviting a wide range of more or less legitimate interests to influence this type of decision making. Another issue is that for the most dedicated among middle-class Malays, halal requirements are by no means fixed or stable but instead elastic and expansive. For these Malays, halal products must also be produced by Muslims to be Islamically acceptable in the wave of halalization. The ongoing nationalization of Islam in Malaysia is discursively driven in that it encompasses constant competition for the most appropriate Islamic practices, pushing and contesting boundaries between the sacred and the profane, and this is clearly the case with regard to food. Evoking the thinking of Durkheim (1995) and Eliade (1987) in their seminal monographs on the sociology of religion, the sacred emerges singularly in binary opposition to its opposite, the profane. The constancy of this struggle actively produces the sacred as a dynamic and negotiable category. The sacralization of certain consumer objects and actions that is taking place in the Islamic field in Malaysia comes into being as an antithesis to the profane, as discussed by Durkheim. For Durkheim (1995: 38), the sacred is generated when lifted out of the context of ordinary, functional human use. Sacred things are protected and isolated by prohibitions and must be separated from the profane. In short, food is a primary marker of class in the interfaces between the state, marketplace, and revivalist Islam in modern Malaysia.

Middle-Class Malays in London

Before entering into the London ethnography in subsequent chapters, I now introduce the larger universe of Malays and Malay(sian) organizations in Britain. I also discuss two significant events that took place during my fieldwork in London. First, these events reflect some of the larger issues of this book and, second, here I met many of my Malay middle-class informants who are essential to the subsequent arguments and discussions.

The lives of Malay seafarers in Liverpool are examples of transnational connections in existence before the global era. This group of Malays were part of extensive maritime networks shaped by the movements of ships and commodities that brought these seafarers to Liverpool. Moreover, from the 1970s onward, Malay students were sent on scholarships to study in the United Kingdom. These groups have become central to state conceptions of national identity in

Malaysia, that is, this sort of "diaspora" is idealized in journalism, the movement called the "Malay World," as well as in academic research, with varying degrees of political patronage. A significant theme relates to the possibility of retaining key traits of Malay culture and identity outside Malaysia while at the same time maintaining links with the homeland. One example of such cultural and religious continuities is newspaper reports about the necessity of the availability of halal meat used in the preparation of Malay food (Bunnell 2007).

In 2006, the Office of National Statistics estimated that there were 1,558,890 Muslims in Britain. The two largest groups are Pakistani (43.2 percent) and Bangladeshi (16.5 percent), whereas "Other Asians" account for 5.8 percent (http://www.statistics.gov .uk/cci/nugget.asp?id=954 and http://www.statistics.gov.uk/cci /nugget.asp?id=957). The Muslim population in London is one of the largest in any European city, and Islam is the second largest religion after Christianity. A total of 607,000 people or 8.5 percent of the population in London identified themselves as Muslim. Forty percent of Muslims in England and Wales live in London (Greater London Authority 2006: 18). In the survey conducted by Greater London Authority in 2006, Malays presumably fit into the "Other" category (29,000 people), but in fact, little is known of this mixed category (Greater London Authority 2006: 23).

According to the Malaysian High Commission in London (personal communication, August 21, 2006), there are about 55,000 Malaysian citizens in the United Kingdom. The distribution of Malays, Chinese, and Indians is unknown. In another personal communication with the Malaysian High Commission (August 6, 2009), I was told that it is most difficult to estimate the currently large number of legal/illegal Malaysians/Malays in the United Kingdom, as these numbers have never been recorded formally. The only credible figure is the British national census carried out in 2001 showing that 49,883 Malaysians were recorded residing in the United Kingdom.

The number of Malaysian students is quite consistent at about 11,800 in recent years. In fact, Malaysian students are the largest group of Southeast Asian overseas students in the United Kingdom (http:// stats.uis.unesco.org/unesco/TableViewer/tableView.aspx?Reportid =171). A large number of Malaysian student organizations exist in the United Kingdom. One of the most prominent is The Malaysian Students Department for the United Kingdom and Eire (www .masduke.net/v3/index.php). Preference is given to the *bumiputera* students in the Malaysian educational system, and in 2006, 76 percent of the top government scholarships were awarded to *bumiputeras* (BERNAMA 2006). In general, the Malaysian educational system can be said to be Malay-centric. Studying in prestigious British universities such as London School of Economics or University College London, students expect to secure a competitive edge in the positional race for jobs, income, and status (Sin 2009: 286). In Malaysia, Malays also enjoy privileges in professional and managerial employment in the civil sector and in commercial and industrial enterprises. This national and transnational Malay-centricity is to a large extent a product of the NEP discussed above as a social engineering policy to support the Malays. Hence, not only the halal vision but indeed also migration processes, education, and work are entangled in complex webs of national and political significance in Malaysia.

Since Britain's colonization of Malaysia, there have been intimate connections and exchanges between the two countries. What is more, Commonwealth migrants from Malaysia could legally settle in Britain. In contemporary Britain, Malays are in most cases in the country to study and/or work. In a broader perspective, the mobility of professionals, executives, technicians, and similarly highly skilled personnel from Asia to developed countries is growing (Castles and Miller 2009: 170).

Many Malay(sian) organizations are active in Britain. To name a few, The British Malaysian Society (www.thebritishmalaysiansociety .org) works for "the enhancement of British Malaysian relations with the aim of promoting business, education and cultural links between Britain and Malaysia." Similarly, the Malay Community Association of the United Kingdom (www.melayu.org) strives to preserve Malay religious identity and culture, on the one hand, and to provide a platform for the considerable number of students in the United Kingdom, on the other.

With regard to trade, London is a gateway to many countries including those with predominantly Muslim populations. The United Kingdom's links with Saudi Arabia, Turkey, Malaysia, Indonesia, and

Pakistan have a trade value of about £15 billion (imports £8.1 billion and exports £6.8 billion). In total, this trade accounts for 2.5 percent of all U.K. trade in goods and services (Greater London Authority 2006: 63). The estimated value of services exported from London to Malaysia is between £100 and £150 million, and the estimated value of goods exported from London is £30–£80 million. Estimated imports from Malaysia to the United Kingdom are estimated at £2 billion and exports from United Kingdom to Malaysia at £1.4 billion (Greater London Authority 2006: 63). These intimate ties are also reflected in the popular media in Malaysia.

This relationship between Malaysia and the United Kingdom is reflected in the newspaper article in *New Straits Times* dated May 29, 2009, with the heading: "No Ordinary Ties." The text reads,

> Malaysia and Britain have a lot to offer each other. Our country has always welcomed British companies and vice versa. British Malaysian Chamber of Commerce (BMCC) chairman and BP Companies Malaysia chief executive officer Datuk [a Malaysian honorary title] Peter M. Wentworth said global British iconic brands operating here include BAE Systems, HSBC, Standard Chartered, Rolls-Royce, BP, Shell, Laura Ashley, Dyson, General Electric, Tesco and TNT. Malaysian interests and investments in the United Kingdom have also blossomed, he added, notably in the oil and gas, water, research and development, leisure and gaming, telecommunications, biotechnology and halal food sectors. Britain remains Malaysia's top three largest trading partner in the European Union and last year bilateral trade stood at US$5.14 billion (RM18 billion) or 12.8 per cent of trade with the EU.

A particular event that took place early in my fieldwork is significant. This event reflects forms of Malay(sian) social, political, and economic organization in a diasporic context. In August 2006, the Malaysian High Commission arranged a Malaysia Day Carnival and UMNO branches from all over the United Kingdom gathered at a Malaysian research center outside London. Each UMNO branch is in charge of a food stall selling (halal) food to a large number of guests (figure 2.1).

In his opening speech, the high commissioner of Malaysia to the United Kingdom declared that to achieve Vision 2020, imagining Malaysia as a fully developed nation by the year 2020, exchanges

Figure 2.1   An UMNO food stall at Malaysia Day Carnival

between the United Kingdom and Malaysia are essential. In the foreword to the *Programme Book* (The Malaysian High Commission 2006: 1) of this event, the high commissioner argues that

> over the years, the Malaysia Day Carnival has been recognised as an event that strengthens the bond of friendship and networking among Malaysians in the United Kingdom [providing] an opportunity for the High Commission, Malaysian private sector and various organisations here in the UK to promote Malaysia.

This network event also involved the Malaysian Business Forum (www.mbf.com.my), as well as the Overseas Malaysian Executive Council (www.my-omec.com) and several producers of Malaysian halal products. Consequently, networking involving state, politics, and food "appears to take the form of highly purposeful and innovative cultivation of actual and implied friendship ties, a micro-strategy along the micro-structures of the corporate and political" (Sloane 1999: 123). At Malaysia Day Carnival, I was not only introduced to the above Malaysian organizations in the diaspora. I also met many of Malay informants at this event that can be said to take place in the interfaces between religion, politics, business, and halal food consumption.

On November 11, 2006, I was at Malaysian Hall in Bayswater, an area of west London that is one of the city's most cosmopolitan areas, for a talk by the managing director of Khasanah Nasional.[3] Malaysia Hall provides accommodation for Malaysian students who have just arrived in London, and it is also the home of the Malaysian Students Department for the United Kingdom and Eire. Several of my informants I knew from Malaysia Day Carnival as well as new ones were present in the audience on this occasion. The scene on which this was played out was a highly formal and "national" conference room with pictures of the Malaysian king, queen, and the present and former UMNO prime ministers as well as the Malaysian national flag. My informants explained to me that the speaker was a very important person who "controls" a lot of funds in the interfaces between the Malaysian state and companies ("government-linked companies" as it were) worldwide. When the speaker entered the room, the organizers humbly bowed, and as the talk was about to start, a few of the participants returned from praying in the prayer room next door.

Convincingly, the managing director discussed visions and initiatives the Malaysian state together with the government-linked companies were, and still are, putting in place to make the best of globalized markets and business opportunities. "Inshallah" (God willing), is added when hopes for a bright economic future for Malaysian national capitalism is expressed. Khazanah Nasional is involved in Malaysian Airlines and the Malaysian car producer Proton symbolizing the technological progress of the nation and the ethnicized state, and the speaker elegantly explained to the audience about how foreign direct investment, human capital, networking, sustainability, and transparency are all essential in the global world of business today. Most of all, it is important to locate strategic "niches in value chains" for Malay(sian) entrepreneurs to exploit, and this is particularly so within Information and Communication Technologies (ICT), tourism and Islamic finance, and halal. Malaysia has a global advantage as an Islamic yet diverse and multiethnic country in which the state has a firm grip on national development. This is particularly the case with Islamic finance and halal. The speaker explained that in the morning, he was praying in an East London mosque where a group of Yemenites had praised Malaysia for its achievements as a highly modern Islamic country in the world today. After this talk, food was served in the adjoining canteen—Malaysian halal cuisine as discussed in this book.

Presentation of Key Informants

It was at the two events discussed above, I met many of my 14 key Malay middle-class informants whose main reason for migrating to Britain was studies and/or work. In many ways, these Malays who all migrated from Kuala Lumpur are comparable with middle-class Malays discussed in my study of proper Islamic consumption in suburban Malaysia. Throughout this book, these informants are essential to the wider discussions and arguments. All the names of informants have been changed. These informants are now introduced in detail to familiarize the reader with their migration narratives and socioeconomic differentiation. The narratives of Malays in London emerge as plotted storylines, narrations, or sequences of events. These narratives embrace halal in the lives of middle-class Malays who migrated from Malaysia to London. Hence, these narratives are truly "spatial trajectories" (de Certeau 1984: 115). In other words, these narratives will be discussed as representatives of the broad class terrain in a diasporic context.

Common to my Malay informants on the frontier is that they are a sophisticated, modern, and cosmopolitan group, that is, they possess what Bourdieu called knowledge of manners or styles as symbolic manifestations that constitute one of the key markers of class. The main point here, however, is to map how objective parameters of class among these middle-class Malays are involved in class practices: a number of different types of capital (economic/cultural/social) and social factors (residence/gender/age/marital status) make up the "specific logic of the field, of what is at stake and the type of capital needed to play for it, which governs those properties through which the relationship between class and practice is established" (Bourdieu

1984: 112–13). These Malays live all across London and not in particular neighborhoods or communities.

It is common to all my informants that they either finished or are in the process of completing tertiary education. Seven of these Malays are currently studying in universities in London such as London School of Economics and University College. Consequently, these Malay students must be economical about their spending in everyday life in expensive London. All these students are in their 20s, and they migrated to London from Kuala Lumpur. Three subjects, economics, political science, and engineering, are favorites with these Malays. Besides studying, much of their time is spent on university-related activities and events such as student organizations and socializing with other students. For the most part, interviews with these informants took place at Malaysian (halal) restaurants around London. Nazli is a single man who came to London in 2001 to study, and he is also a student councilor with an Islamic student organization. He lives with 15 other students in a hall of residence in central London. Alina moved to London in 2005 together with her husband Hasan. They live in a small flat in South London. Together with the next informant, Zurina, Alina was the only informant who wore the *tudung* (long headscarf). None of my other informants would wear Islamic dress or grow a *janggut* (beard) symbolizing piety, for example. Zurina is a single woman who came to London in 2005. She lives with three flatmates in South London. Fatimah is a single woman who had lived in London since 2005. Besides studying, she works for a phone company. Fatimah shares a flat with two friends in North London. Usmirah and Henny arrived in London in 2005, and they share a flat in central London close to their university.

Another group of middle-class Malays already finished their tertiary education in Malaysia or Britain and now work in London. Common to this group is a stable financial situation, and several of these informants have children. Abdul is a 29-year-old man, and he lives with his wife and their child in a house in Colindale in north London. He moved to Britain in 1996 to study accountancy, and he now works as an accountant. Binsar is a single man in his 30s and has lived in London since 1995. He moved there to study and now works as an architect. He lives with a friend in a flat in central London.

Murni is a man in his 20s. He is married to Altaf who is about the same age, and the couple moved to London in 1998 to study, and they now both work in the financial sector. The couple lives in a house in Walthamstow in northeast London. Irfan is a 29-year-old man who moved to London in 1994 to finish his schooling as a medical doctor, and he now works in a hospital. He lives in a flat that he borrowed from a friend in central London. Kamaruddin is a single man in his 50s, who left Malaysia in the 1970s to study engineering in Singapore. Since then, he has traveled extensively in many parts of Asia and Europe, and now he lives permanently in London where he works for engineering companies. He lives in a flat in Earl's Court, central London.

Finally, Mascud is a Malay *imam* in his 30s, who moved from Kuala Lumpur to London in 2002 where he works as a religious councilor at Malaysia Hall, a facility that provides accommodation for Malaysian students who have just arrived in London. At Malaysia Hall, there is also a canteen where Malaysian halal dishes are served. This work with introducing students to living in Britain includes guidance on proper halal food practice. Mascud is married with two children. He studied Arabic literature in Morocco and did his master's at the University of Malaya in Kuala Lumpur, Malaysia's largest university.

Halal understanding and practice among these middle-class Malays is inseparable from this chapter's discussion of how the Malay middle class emerged in the interfaces between revivalist Islam, state, and market. My study in 2001–2002 discussed above demonstrated that halal consumption is entangled in evermore-complex webs of political, ethnic, and national significance in modern Malaysia. These transformations are tightly linked to the emergence of Malay aesthetic communities. Notions of the sacred in Malaysia have taken on more political meanings, and I propose to see the proliferation of halal as a type of national standardization that attempts to achieve legibility and simplification. At the same time, the state in Malaysia strategically employs halal as a material sign to overcome critiques of excessive secularism and as an ethnic marker vis-à-vis the Chinese and "bad Malay" other. Food consumption and its religious, social, and cultural context may be the closest one can come to a core symbol in the everyday lives of the Malay middle class. Capitalism is adjusting to the recent requirements of a growing number of Muslims, and the Islamic market is expanding rapidly, that is, in the new millennium halalization also signifies a type of globalized religious market that covers new types of commodities and services, as it is the case in contemporary London.

Chapter 3

Between Halal and the Secular in London[1]

Outside Southeast Asia, London is emerging as a center for halal production, trade, and consumption. At the same time, the meaning and
practices of halal are being transformed and contested. Paradoxically,
in the eyes of many Muslims in Britain, this proliferation of halal calls
attention to a form of impotent secular government, that is, in the
eyes of some Malays, for example, "secular food" in Britain is a sign
of the state's unwillingness or incapacity to recognize the demands of
religious consumers. Arguably, the frontiers of government should be
"rolled forward" to protect consumers in the expanding halal market.
In other words, the more the culture of Islamic consumption asserts
itself and halal is globalized and delocalized as a religious market,
the more the state's incapacity to define what is legitimate halal and,
thus, the unity of Islam is felt. Hence, modern and delocalized halal is
pushing and challenging the frontier between "the secular" and secular government, on the one hand, and religion, on the other hand.

I show that among the Malays, halal evokes a range of sensibilities,
attitudes, assumptions, and behavior that may support or undermine
"the secular" as an epistemic category in everyday life. I will also
explore how diverse migration narratives of my informants condition
particular understandings and practices of halal. I argue that modern forms of halal consumption in London challenge and reconfigure
what are often considered separate secular realms of state, government, and politics, on the one hand, and the intimacy of religious life
and expression, on the other.

In this and the following chapters, I examine the workings of the state in Malaysia and Britain through the halal understanding and practice of my Malay informants. At the same time, "diaspora experiences and discourses are entangled, never clear of commodification" (Clifford 1994: 313). My study is also an exploration of a microdimension of transnationalism (Guarnizo and Smith 1998: 26). A central theme is how Islamic organizations in Britain claim authority through halal in the interfaces between expanding religious markets, the secular, and the rights and demands of a growing group of Muslim consumers.

"Doubled in Size for 2006"? The Halal Hype in London

In November 2005, the Halal Exhibition at the major World Food Market (WFM) in London was held for the first time. The venue was ExCeL London, a huge exhibition and conference center in London's Docklands, an area in the southeastern part of the city that has been redeveloped principally for commercial and residential use. In addition to the large number of booths displaying halal products, WFM also offered seminars on the business potential of halal in the rapidly expanding "ethnic food" or "world food" market.

A large number of booths sold a wide variety of fresh, chilled, and frozen halal food products such as meat/poultry, sausages, samosas, kebabs, bread, fast food, baby food, nuts, and dry fruits. Candy in these booths included fruit gum made with fish gelatin and chocolate bars. Halal drinks were also displayed—fruit drinks, Mecca-Cola (promoted as an Islamically correct cola that is an alternative to the imperialist megabrands), and what appeared to be Zamzam water. Zamzam water is marketed as a sacred source of water from God coming from the Well of Zamzam located near the holiest place in Mecca, the *Kaaba* (the square building inside the great mosque in Mecca, containing a sacred black stone). Nonfood halal products were also displayed, for example, NewGenn cleaning and disinfection for use especially in food preparation. As we shall see, some of these products are certified with logos displaying and identifying the certifier, but many are not. Besides the Halal Exhibition, the WFM also included a Kosher Exhibition and an Ethnic & Speciality Food

Exhibition. The Ethnic & Specialty section is placed in a middle position separating the halal and kosher sections. These different zones are clearly marked on the map over the WFM one receives before entering. Hence, halal is marked on the map of the exhibition. In many cases halal marks the single booths, and is written on products (in Arabic and/or Roman characters).

The quotation in this heading refers to a claim made in the *Official Show Guide* promoting the WFM held in 2006 in London, namely that compared with 2005 this event had "doubled in size for 2006." This exhibition may have "doubled in size," but this statement also reflects a broader halal hype in London. A large number of companies and Islamic organizations are represented at the Halal Exhibition, each having a particular understanding of what can be considered proper halal consumption. WFM stresses the point that "it is in the exchange and public display of food and feasts and festivals that the politics of food comes into full force" (Manderson 1986a: 15).

In 2006, a delegation from the Malaysia External Trade Development Corporation (MATRADE) had a booth at the Halal Exhibition. In 2006, I attended both Malaysia International Halal Showcase (MIHAS) and WFM. In a way, the Halal Exhibition and the various groups and organizations participating in it bring out how the proliferation of halal sits uneasily between Islamic revivalism, commercialization, and "the secular" as an epistemic category in everyday life.

The controversial question of halal certification surfaced on the first day of the WFM seminars. A former director of environmental health and consumer affairs services who was also an advisor to the London Central Mosque on halal questions accused many of the companies present of promoting halal products that were not properly halal certified by an Islamic authority.

To this advisor, the lack of a state body in Britain that is capable of inspecting the "totally unregulated" halal market has left this market open to fraud, corruption, and without any kind of standards, uniform certification, or legislation. This, in turn, is distorting the commercially promoted image of halal as healthy, pure, and modern in an era of food scares. In the eyes of this advisor and many Malays in London, the Jewish system of kosher certification is seen

as a model for the institutionalization, standardization, and certification of halal in the gray zones between religious revivalism, the
state, and consumer culture. Similar to halal, kosher is certified by
Jewish organizations, and the state is not involved in these processes.
For some Malays in London, kosher is an acceptable and accessible
choice if halal food for some reason is not within reach. Some products may even be both halal and kosher certified. However, as alcohol
is acceptable according to kosher rules, some Malays check labels to
see whether a kosher product contains alcohol or not.

Present at WFM were numerous Islamic organizations, groups, and
individuals who understand and practice halal in divergent ways. An
example of such an organization is the Halal Food Authority (HFA)[2]
(www.halalfoodauthority.co.uk), an organization set up in 1994 to
certify halal meat, and to which, I shall return below. Second, a number of government institutions, such as schools and hospitals, were
represented in that they are experiencing an increase in halal sensibilities among Muslim groups. In fact, a number of London hospitals
provide halal meals (Greater London Authority 2006: 75).

Third, several market research firms specializing in "ethnic markets" participated to provide in-depth understanding of the transformation of halal. Finally, a large number of Muslim consumers were
there to learn how modern understandings and practices of halal are
being transformed.

In the eyes of the MATRADE delegation at the Halal Exhibition
mentioned above, the United Kingdom, and London in particular,
is potentially an extremely lucrative market. London qualifies as a
"global city" (Sassen 2002: 2), that is, London plays an important
role in linking the national economy with global circuits, and this is
also the case with halal. At this exhibition, I discussed the halal potential of this market with a young Malay Muslim woman, Jeti, who, as
stated in the previous chapter, I knew from attending MIHAS, in
Malaysia earlier in 2006. She is currently involved in promoting halal
in Britain for the Malaysian state through her private company. She
is an example of a Malaysian entrepreneur with a global orientation,
and she represents a modern type of Malay diasporic group privileged
by the Malaysian state. The Malaysian state financially supported
her education and her promotion of halal in Britain. In return, the

state expects these highly educated Malay Muslim entrepreneurs to embody a modern type of Islamic diaspora on the global stage.

Understandings and practices of halal among diasporic Malays are incomprehensible without comparing Malaysia and Britain as two countries in which "the secular" are signs of quite different trajectories and meanings. In other words, my focus is on how Malay diasporic groups consume and negotiate halal in the interfaces between powerful Malaysian state discourses, the secular state and Islamic organizations in Britain, and the commercialization of halal.

I argue that we should unpack the various assumptions that constitute "secularism" as a political doctrine. Moreover, current meanings associated with secularism have come to embody much more than the progression from religion to secularism (Asad 2003: 1). From its origin in modern Euro-America, secularism in its most simple form represented an idealization of separating religious from secular institutions in government (Asad 2003: 1). My main focus is on "the secular" as comprising concepts, practices, and sensibilities that conceptually are prior to secularism (Asad 2003: 16). The secular is ubiquitous in modern life and not easily grasped, so it may most fruitfully be "pursued through its shadows" (Asad 2003: 16).

My exploration of halal in everyday life among Malays in London provides ethnographic specificity to meanings and practices associated with "the secular" and secular government as part of divergent state practices in Malaysia and Britain. In the majority of debates about secularism, "there is an unfortunate tendency to understand the secular state in rather undifferentiated terms: modern, homogenizing and driven by objectifying scientific modes of governance" (Hansen 2000: 255). Unpacking secularism involves a focus on how middle-class Malays live "the secular" and divergent modes of secular government in everyday life, as I shall show in the case of halal.

Secular Bodies in Britain?

As could be expected, the standardization, bureaucratization, and certification of halal in Malaysia are in contrast with the far more fragmented and complex halal market in Britain as a frontier on which a plethora of groups, organizations, and individuals have divergent ideas about halal. So far, scholarly attention to halal in Britain for the most part has focused on conflicts over the provision of halal in schools (Abbas 2005) and the politics of religious slaughter (Charlton and Kaye 1985; Kaye 1993). In many parts of London, such as Edgware Road, Finsbury Park, and Whitechapel Road, halal is a distinctive presence on signs and in butcher shops and restaurants. Lately, halal-certified products in large numbers are appearing in supermarkets such as Tesco and Asda (a British supermarket chain that retails both food and merchandise). In effect, the novel ubiquity of halal in some parts of London can be seen as a form of urban space making (Metcalf 1996) and Islamic visibility (Esposito 2003: 195). I shall return to this aspect in Chapter 5. Simultaneously, religion in Britain is experiencing a renewed political importance.

Egalitarian multiculturalism builds on the idea that identities are partly given shape or denied by the recognition or nonrecognition of others: "Due recognition is not just a courtesy we owe people. It is a vital human need" (Taylor 1994: 26). More specifically, there is a demand, as in the case of halal, for public institutions to acknowledge "ways of doing things" (Modood 2005: 134) privately and publicly.

In Britain, secular government predominates at a cultural level in the context of institutionally complex ties between church and state (Fetzer and Soper 2005: 38), and the arrival of Muslims disclosed these intimate ties, so that over time Islamic practices have been recognized (Fetzer and Soper 2005: 61). In other words, Muslim migration is a test for the inherited church-state establishment (Fetzer and Soper 2005: 17). At the same time, "contemporary London's cultural diversity is the product of a global migration dominated by those from Britain's former empire" (Eade 2000: 180), as it is the case with Malays and Malaysia. In Britain, the constitution does not establish religious rights as fundamental. Instead, religious rights are left to the political arena (Fetzer and Soper 2005: 35). However, the state in Britain "extends rights and privileges to specific religious communities, usually Christian, particularly in the social service and education public policy sectors" (Fetzer and Soper 2005: 17).

During my fieldwork in London in 2006, several Labour Party ministers criticized and questioned Muslim women's right to wear the *niqab* (a veil that covers the face). One headline read, "This Veil

Fixation Is Doing Muslim Women No Favours": "We need an honest debate about women and Islam. But the current politically driven campaign is making that more difficult" (*Guardian*, October 19, 2006). Another heading was "Tribunal Dismisses Case of Muslim Woman Ordered Not to Teach in Veil" (*Guardian*, October 20, 2006). Finally, in the article "White Pupils Less Tolerant," a survey shows the point was made that "arguments about the Muslim veil in Britain are part of a wider debate taking place across Europe. Amid competing claims of religious freedom and official secularism, some argue that the debate is motivated by growing intolerance of Muslims" (*Guardian*, October 21, 2006). Thus, the veil is essentialized as "Muslim culture" and thought to establish a "community" with shared values despite ethnic, national, and linguistic diversity (Bauman 1996: 23). The *Sunday Times* (October 22, 2006) asked, "Is It Time to Take God Out of the State?":

> Faith groups are increasingly demanding new rights or complaining of being wronged. Some say the time has come for Britain to create a clear divide between state and religion. Are they right? Religion, long dormant as a force in British politics and society, is back. After 9/11 and 7/7, rows over niqabs, hijabs, Christian crosses, faith schools and dress codes have exposed deep rifts in our attitudes to the spiritual.

Conversely, some British Muslims and organizations call upon the state to help recognize and standardize halal. Contrary to the intense debate over veiling, there is no corresponding state discourse on halal in Britain. Apparently, more conventional forms of secularism as political doctrine define the secular in everyday life in terms of overt dressing on or of Muslim bodies, whereas more covert halal consumption in these bodies is seen to be uncontroversial. What is more, the state plays a central role in the governance of London itself (Travers 2004: 13) but not with regard to governing religious markets in the city. Many Muslims in London consider the city a frontier wilderness that is in need of governance.

Slaughter in accordance to Islamic law has been permitted in the United Kingdom under the Slaughter of Animals Act of 1933 (Charlton and Kaye 1985: 490) and Slaughterhouses Act 1974 (Charlton and Kaye 1985: 495), which expressly permit the slaughter of animals without prior stunning.[3] Animals' rights groups see these laws as inhuman, and controversies over the Jewish and Muslim slaughter of animals for food have surfaced periodically during the twenty-first century (Charlton and Kaye 1985; Kaye 1993; Lewis 1994; Vertovec 1996: 170). However, early interactions between Britain and Asia included three Moroccan delegations visiting London in the seventeenth century, and for the first time, civil servants were faced with the question of halal meat provision (Greater London Authority 2006: 14).

The hostility to religious slaughter "heightened awareness of Islamic practice and a sense of self-identity among a growing number of British Muslims" (Ansari 2004: 355). In this respect, the state recognizes religious needs and adopted policies to accommodate Muslim groups. However, as the understanding and practice of halal production, trade, and consumption are being transformed to involve more and more types of products, not unlike the way this has already happened to kosher products, the state is called upon to help regulate these commodities. Although the state in Britain recognizes traditional halal requirements such as religious slaughter without stunning, it has virtually no authority to inspect, certify, or standardize halal. In the eyes of some British Muslims, this leaves consumers unprotected against growing commercial interest in halal.

Claiming Authority through Halal

I discussed above how a former director of environmental health and consumer affairs services who is also an advisor to the London Central Mosque at WFM critiques products promoted here for not being properly certified. In front of a large audience at the WFM seminar in 2006, he made it clear that there is a large market for fraud and corruption within the halal trade and in the local certifying bodies such as HFA and Halal Monitoring Committee (HMC) (www.halalmc .co.uk)—both represented in the audience at this seminar. He called for the Muslim community to "wake up" and "clean up their act." Finally, the advisor declared that the state authorities may be willing to "take somebody to court" and "take enforcement action," but these bodies "feel that the Muslim community has not decided yet what the definition of halal is in the first place." As it were, so-called expert certifiers, for example, *imams* without any real knowledge of halal, were issuing certificates "as long as the money is sent first." Consequently, to standardize this "totally unregulated" market, he requested the government and the Food Standards Agency[4] "to give us a hand so that we can come up with something like standards against which halal food can be inspected."

These views are supported by Dr. Yunes Teinaz, who is a health advisor to the director general at the Islamic Cultural Centre in London. For 10 years, he has worked on illegal food and brought cases to court. When we discussed halal and law in his office in Hackney, a borough in north London, he explained to me that "you can easily buy certification if you pay for it. And they get away with it because there is no control, regulation, or inspection from the state." In Britain, there is no food legislation that is specific to halal (Pointing, Teinaz, and Shafi 2008: 206). The Muslim Council of Britain (MCB), an interest group, warns that up to 90 percent of the meat and poultry sold to be halal in the United Kingdom may have been sold illegally and not slaughtered according to the requirements of Muslims. Supermarkets such as Asda, Morrisons (the fourth-largest chain of supermarkets in the United Kingdom) and Sainsbury's (the third-largest chain of supermarkets in the United Kingdom) are marketing their halal meat as 100 percent halal authorized by HFA (Ahmed 2008: 656).

As halal and the aspect of religious slaughter increasingly infused Muslim identity in Britain, the need to establish a body of halal butcher shops was recognized. Consequently, in 1994, the HFA was set up with encouragement from the Muslim Parliament of Great Britain, a pan-Muslim interest group, and HFA established a network of approved abattoirs and shops to provide the community with independently certified halal meat (Ansari 2004: 355).

Contrary to the Jewish certification and institutionalization of kosher, the approach to halal among Muslims in Britain has been more fragmented and disunited, and "the broad range of emerging political demands may have served to dilute organizational effectiveness" (Kaye 1993: 251). Moreover, Muslim organizations in Britain claiming to represent the Muslim community are of relatively recent origin and often lack both resources and political experience (Kaye 1993: 247).

As we have seen, this call for halal standards is to a large extent modeled on Jewish kosher certification. Jewish groups in the United Kingdom have been more concerted in their effort to impose these requirements, and they have thus been recognized by the state to a larger extent.

Interestingly, the current situation in Britain is somewhat similar to that of Malaysia prior to state recognition and regulation of "national" halal starting in the early 1980s. What some Muslim groups call for is such a national standard for halal that can mark a kind of British Muslim unity and identity. The central difference, of course, is that the secular state in Britain is reluctant to extend recognition of a relatively fragmented halal market beyond already existing regulation on food in general.

HFA is a "voluntary, non-profit making organization" (www.halalfoodauthority.co.uk) set up in 1994 to license

> slaughterhouses, distribution centres, retailers and providers of meat and poultry for human consumption. These licenses are granted on an annual and contractual basis. The HFA inspectors are there to audit and monitor compliance of both Islamic laws and MAFF (Ministry of Agriculture, Fisheries and Food.) and EU regulations of slaughter. The HFA is also assiduously engaged in regulating, endorsing and authenticating food stuffs, pharmaceuticals, confectionary, toiletries, flavourings, emulsifiers, colourings…for Muslim usage. (www.halalfoodauthority.co.uk)

In an increasingly complex food market, these activities seem bold for a voluntary organization. Interestingly, the intentions and activities of HFA take place in the interfaces between not only the secular and the religious but apparently also local, national and international organizations, and forms of legislation on food. From my conversation with the HFA president, information on the organization's website, and the president's attendance at WFM, it is clear that halal is formative of more and more "network events" indicating the emergence of a global halal "network" or "community." For example, we learn that the president attends a large number of national and international halal seminars, and the speeches delivered are there for us to see on the website. In fact, the president attended the International Muslim Trade Exhibition held in 1998 in Kuala Lumpur. Similar to the way in which the Malaysian state is claiming authority through halal, HFA is "regulating, endorsing and authenticating halal" (www.halalfoodauthority.co.uk).

With reference to halal in Malaysia, the HFA president made it clear to me that contrary to HFA, Jabatan Kemajuan Islam Malaysia or the Islamic Development Department of Malaysia (JAKIM) that was set up to regulate halal is "supervised and works under government instruction." Only "reluctantly" does JAKIM recognize the work of HFA as a nongovernmental organization. Unlike Malaysia, where halal is a major prestige project supported financially by the state, HFA is independently "generating" its funds through fees paid for audit by slaughterhouses and cutting plants.

When I visited HFA, there seemed to be a discrepancy between its visions, ambitions, and policies stated on the organization's website and the modest office facilities in London housing the organization's limited number of staff. My point here is that halal is a significant field for claiming recognition in a fragmented religious market, whereas practices of regulating halal are highly resource demanding. At WFM in 2005 and 2006, the HFA president was also present and so was the vice-chairman of the HMC. HMC was established in 2003 in Leicester, and contrary to HFA, it is against the stunning of animals before slaughter. These two organizations can be seen as competitors with overlapping interests and claims for authority in the halal market.

When discussing these issues with Nazli at Malaysia Hall (see below), where he was involved in voluntary work for The Malaysian Students Department for the United Kingdom and Eire, he, for one, said it bluntly that most of all, halal in the United Kingdom is about politics and business. He explained to me that a lot of ethnic politics is involved in halal in the United Kingdom with the Arabs acting as "gatekeepers" while there is no centralized monitoring of this market in existence.

In fact, many informants see the proliferation of halal in the United Kingdom as an overwhelmingly commercial endeavor for which Islam is a vehicle that was pragmatically employed by Islamic organizations, nations, and the halal industry. Hence, as halal is delocalized, it is affected by distant affairs.

However, the HFA president objects to this form of commercial-ization of halal and maintains that there is a distinctive religious or ethical aspect to halal as well. This is a significant point because in the current halal market, a large part of the production and trade is car-ried out by non-Muslims. So maintaining that there is a definite reli-gious aspect to halal is also a way of linking halal to Muslim groups and their interests.

A large part of the research into halal in the United Kingdom is carried out by "secular" market research companies such as Mintel (www.mintel.com) and Ethnic Focus (www.ethnicfocus.com) that are starting to recognize the commercial aspects of halal. The HFA president critiques Mintel's overly commercial approach to halal, but at the same time, supermarkets in London such as Tesco and Asda require products that are halal certified by locally recognized bodies such as HFA and HMC. In this way, halal is being lifted out of its traditional base in halal butchers' shops to become part of "world food" ranges in major supermarkets.

Islamic organizations in Britain claim authority through and com-pete over halal in the interfaces between expanding markets, the sec-ular, and the rights and demands of Muslim consumers. At the same time, these organizations push for a form of national halal standard, which could be seen as a sign of Muslim unity and identity. So far, these organizations have not been able to unite Muslim groups around a shared vision of standards. As more and more products appear in this expanding market, both Islamic organizations and commercial interests compete over standards and certification in the margins of the secular state. The emergence of this type of Islamic consumption draws attention to the state's incapacity to regulate halal and thus recognize a Muslim "community." The question is how Malays in London navigate this market in terms of halal understanding and practice.

"You Just Have to Shut One Eye": Halal in Malay Migration Narratives

This section serves as an introduction to middle-class Malay under-standings of halal in London with particular attention to the role of delocalized halal and the power and authority the Malaysian state evokes in the diaspora. Although this discussion is mainly based on the testimonies of my informants, subsequent chapters also map everyday halal practices of middle-class Malays in greater ethnographic detail. Here, it suffices to say that as halal is globalized or delocalized as a religious market, proper halal practice is becoming evermore contested. An example of a contested question among Malays is to what extent halal should or should not apply only to meat. Another contested issue is whether halal is important in the context of non-food products. On a number of websites and blogs Malays often use in London, proper halal understanding and practice is open to a variety of interpretations. As we shall see, some Malays are quite relaxed about halal in the diaspora, whereas others are far more fastidious. However, these sentiments should all be explored on the backdrop of halal's forceful history and transformation in the Malaysian context of Islamic revivalism, state standardization, and market forces. In many cases, halal ideas and ideals are not easily translated into actual practices in the diasporic context.

Three narratives dominated Malay halal sentiments. First, Malay concern about halal can be ascribed to the relatively strict *Shafi'i* school of jurisprudence within the Sunni division of Islam dominant in Malaysia. While enjoying a meal in a Malaysian restaurant in London's West End, Alina explained to me that

> I would always say that Malaysian Muslims are stricter. It is just the way that we were taught, I think. We are Sunni, Shafi'i school of thought, we are the strictest. Even if you go to Mecca there are a lot of people who pray differently, or eat differently, they say that this is considered halal, but for us it is not halal. I have Pakistani friends here in London and they still go to Kentucky Fried Chicken and eat the chicken, they don't care. I guess to them if you have been in a country for a long time you can eat whatever in that country whether it's halal or not.

Hasan in the same restaurant agrees that halal fastidiousness is endemic to the *Shafi'i* school of thought. Still, this couple (students on a relatively low budget in expensive London) would sometimes eat meat from discount supermarkets such as the German-owned Lidl despite what they considered insufficient or unconvincing certification.

Second, on several occasions, I had the opportunity to discuss halal with a Malay *imam*, Mascud, who has lived in London with his family since 2002. He was working at Malaysia Hall. The facility provides accommodation for Malaysian students who have just arrived in London, and there is also a canteen at the Hall where Malaysian halal dishes are served. His work of introducing students to living in Britain includes guidance on proper halal food practice. Mascud can be seen as a kind of Islamic bureaucrat in a diasporic context. In his view, Malays living with non-Muslim Chinese in Malaysia may sharpen Malay alertness to contamination from nonhalal sources. To Mascud, this apprehension about the food habits of the other was also significant in a British context where general indifference about food clearly contrasted with Malay particularity. Mascud explained that several Chinese had told him that the Chinese are compelled to eat pork everyday, even in "vegetarian food."

In London, there are a large number of Chinese restaurants, takeaways, et cetera, many of which display some form of halal sign or logo on their door. Among Malay informants, as we shall see, these restaurants are generally not considered halal. First, some informants believe that Chinese restaurants simply cannot be halal.

From previous research in Malaysia, I had learned that it is often rumored among Malays that, despite Malay requirements and sensitivity, the Chinese use lard in food production and cooking. The owner of a Malaysian restaurant in London, who was extremely alert to halal requirements and only employed Malays, complained about one of the other Malaysian restaurants in London owned by a Chinese person. Even though the restaurant displayed a halal sign, alcohol was available in the restaurant's bar. Moreover, no Malays were employed there, and, most importantly, on several occasions, Malaysian ministers, even the prime minister, were said to have frequented this establishment on their visits to London. As a consequence, the immoral practices of the political elite are seen as undermining the state discourse on halal. Moreover, employing Chinese and not Malays is unpatriotic and unsupportive of the vision to create a Malay diaspora or halal network. In this way, halal is expressive of powerful forms of ethnic distinctions between Malays and Chinese. I met up with Malays at this restaurant who did not object. One of these Malays was Alina, who can be considered fastidious about halal. My point here is that no matter how strict or fastidious middle-class Malays in London may be about halal sentiments, these are in many cases open to nego-tiation and not necessarily translated into systematic practices. This point adds to the multiplicity and ambiguity that is often involved in halal understanding and practice.

Third, there was a forceful impact from schooling, and thus the state, involving information about halal as part of the school system in Malaysia. In their narratives, most informants gave details that such basic and extended knowledge of halal is part of their school experience. As could be expected, halal knowledge and practice was generated and transmitted in families, but halal within the school system was far more pronounced in informants' accounts.

Hasan's basic knowledge of halal was taught both in "normal" school and in Islamic school in Malaysia. In Malaysia, Islamic teach-ings within the school system are state regulated, and this point is evident in Alina's account below. Moreover, Alina argues that the effects of the relationship between family and state give shape to halal understanding and practice. Alina:

> Parents teach you about halal on a day-to-day basis. If you actually go to a religious school it is more, you know, in-depth. In normal school you have religious studies as well, so it is the same thing, it is not just religious school, it is religion. Throughout the years since you are in the primary school, first grade till you are 17. The basic things that we were taught at home are not to eat pork and alcohol. That is the basics, every Muslim should actually know that. But the other stuff you have to actually learn about it. You know like whether you can eat certain seafoods, which live in water in the other world. We have to learn to know. It is like crabs, some of the crabs you can actually eat and some you can't. It is exactly like alligators, they live in a different world, both in water and outside as well, like frogs, we can't eat frogs.

To this, Hasan added that the question of halal is addressed in "one class, one course, compulsory." These statements testify to the fact that halal is a type of state-regulated taxonomy in modern Malaysia that is articulated between families and schools and, thus, the state. At the same time, these sentiments show how halal may give shape to an aesthetic community that is intertwined with a moral community.

Other younger informants, Abdul for example, refer to this type of knowledge as a natural part of "a national curriculum" or a "common understanding." However, Abdul during our discussion at a Malaysian halal restaurant in Edgware Road stressed that even though the knowledge of halal was taught or presented as part of a national curriculum, this was mainly "theory" or a sign of idealized behavior by school and religious authorities that he and his friends would not "apply" in any systematic way. Hence, halal is open to forms of mitigation that may undermine or question state authority.

To Nazli, the transmission of halal knowledge within the school system in Malaysia is part of a "general knowledge" or "a syllabus," and similarly, Zurina outlines halal in the school system in the following way:

> At seven you are being taught that basic stuff about how to pray and not about halal until you are older and it's more concentrated, in-depth. I remember I learned about halal when I was 15 or 16 years old.

In this way, experiencing religion at home and in schooling, in "private" spaces, "is crucial to the formation of subjects who will eventually inhabit a particular public culture" (Asad 2003: 185). It is these experiences from Malaysia that give shape to Malays' understanding and practice of halal in London.

Younger informants told a story about leaving the haven of Malaysia to study or work in London where a good dose of pragmatism was necessary in Muslim food consumption. Abdul's words, which are part of the heading of this section, pinpoint the sentiment that when you live your life outside Malaysia and halal availability is unsatisfactory, "you just have to shut one eye." For example, a pragmatic strategy or practice would be simply to consume halal products that may be suspected of not being halal and buy kosher products or vegetarian food. For most Malays, everyday pragmatism was the order of the day when living abroad and without the imagined safety of JAKIM-certified products. However, compared with Abdul, Alina and Zurina, for example, are far more fastidious about halal, and they do not simply trust halal sellers' claims. Hence, in a diasporic context outside the realm of the Malaysian state, the more fastidious Malays desire extensive knowledge about halal sellers. Conversely, more relaxed Malays pragmatically trust these sellers "in good faith."

Islamic revivalist critiques of "secularism" and the "secular state/ government" in Malaysia have helped shape and reinforce not only a unique type of powerful United Malays National Organisation (UMNO)-driven nationalism but also a highly commercialized version of Islam in which halal plays a significant role.

In contrast, secular government in Britain is reluctant to extend recognition of a relatively fragmented halal market beyond already existing regulation on food in general. For example, Mascud told me that medication in London might contain pork gelatin without this being stated on the label. Most of all, however, in the eyes of the *imam* and many informants as we shall see in the subsequent chapters, halal is unconvincing in Britain because the secular government has no authority to carry out inspections, unlike JAKIM. He argues that even in Malaysia, the reliability of JAKIM inspections can be questioned because this body is responsible for "monitoring" the entire country. The point here is that in Malaysia, many Malays are well aware that these inspections are symbolic practices of the ethnicized state involved in legitimizing halal. In praxis, it would be impossible to verify halal in every single product.

Conversely, in Britain due to the lack of state involvement in halal, trusting individual halal producers, traders, and butchers is essential. By far, informants preferred Malaysian state-certified products if these were readily available. Informants recognize the halal logo issued by JAKIM on these products from their everyday lives in Malaysia. State-certified halal in Malaysia is described as "familiar," "trustworthy," "reliable," and "convincing." Some informants argue that state certification is more reliable because producers only pay a small fee for certification, whereas certifying bodies in Britain were "profiting" from certification. As a consequence, the Malaysian state appears to be more dedicated to the Islamic ethos in halal rather than the commercial aspects involved in nonstate certification.

Comparatively, older informants such as Kamaruddin who had been living outside Malaysia for a longer period of time were not equally exposed to Malaysian state halal. Kamaruddin sees himself as "a flexible Muslim" who willingly had escaped the politicized piety and excessive focus on proper Muslim consumption of modern Malaysia. He is quite unaffected by the bureaucratization of Malay

Muslim identities that has taken place in Malaysia since the 1970s. In Malaysia at that time, halal was mainly about trusting the authority of the local halal butcher shop, he told me when we met at a pub in London's West End. Interestingly, this story about shopping for halal in Malaysia in the 1970s is comparable with younger Malays' accounts of contemporary shopping for halal meat in local butcher shops in London.

Malay migration narratives condition particular halal understandings and practices. I have shown how modern forms of halal consumption in London blur what is often considered separate secular realms of state and politics, on the one hand, and the intimacy of religious life and expression, on the other. To many Malays, a lack of state regulation of halal, for example, with reference to meat and labeling, in the public realm leaves much to be desired. This, in turn, produces a kind of pragmatic personalization and privatization of halal understanding and practice. These sentiments should be seen on the backdrop of the Malaysian state's effort to instill halal as nationalized and authoritative understanding and practice in Malay consumers. Nazli, who is a student councilor with an Islamic student organization in London, argued that sensibility to halal is crucial as "Malays, Muslims we believe that what becomes part of your body stays on. So it is very important that you make sure it is the right things."

In London, Malays live at the margin of the Malaysian state, that is, in a space between bodies, law, and discipline (Das and Poole 2004: 10). At the same time, this state has helped create this group of New Malays and has encouraged and supported their stay in London—to mend the "diaspora-envy" of the state. In the case of Malaysian halal, on the one hand, sovereign power exercised by the state disciplines Muslim bodies and, on the other, these modern forms of Islamic bureaucratization recognize Malay ethnicity. Moreover, this disciplining is reinforced by the globalization of halal as a religious market that is taking place. However, "A state may be sovereign..., but that doesn't dispense with, it intensifies, the requirements to make *sure* of itself....the modern state's authority passes straight off the edge of the graspable, immediately knowable world" (Rose 1996: 8). Halal in Malay migration trajectories is a sign of tangibility and materiality of stateness. The consumption of Malaysian state-certified halal products in London is a form of state sovereignty in the diaspora. The state in Malaysia decided to regulate halal to control Islamic expression among Malays, and it is this strategy of preemption that today bolsters, naturalizes, and enhances state authority among middle-class Malays. Hansen and Stepputat write that

> proliferating "diasporas" crystallize in diverse transnational entrepreneurial networks, and cultural, religious, and political organizations and often receive handsome backing from governments in the nation-states of their origin. There are successful attempts not only to retain loyalty and secure remittances from transnationalized citizens but also to assert the sovereignty of the nation-state beyond its territorial boundaries. (2005: 33)

At the same time, delocalized halal is entangled in complex webs of political significance, social practice, discourse, controversy, and conventions. A concrete example of how political economy and regulation condition actual halal consumption is that due to EU regulations, Malaysia is not allowed to export (halal) meat products to the European Union and Britain. Hence, as JAKIM certified meat is not available, Malays must look for other types of certification. I have shown how political doctrines of "secularism" in Malaysia and Britain are often blurred in the gray zones between religious revivalism, the state, and consumer culture. Comparing halal as a particular field of understanding and practice in these two countries reflects widely different religious and secular attitudes toward the human body.

The state in Malaysia is trying to preempt *dakwah* critiques of a "secular" state. In response, the state bureaucratized, standardized, and nationalized a Malaysian version of Islam and halal. These processes produce novel forms of management of life in terms of proper Islamic conduct and a whole range of sentiments, sensibilities, and anxieties associated with everyday consumption. These concerns are prominent among Malays in Malaysia but even more so among Malays in London.

To some extent, the state in Britain has accommodated claims, for example, rights to religious slaughter. However, the growing focus on modern halal among producers and consumers has drawn attention to the misrecognition of halal among some groups of

Muslims—especially vis-à-vis kosher recognition. In effect, the state in Britain is seen as passive and strangely uninvolved in an expanding market.

In Britain, competing Islamic organizations are trying to standardize or "monitor" halal. These organizations are faced with difficulties as a plethora of Muslim groups understand and practice halal differently based on different schools of Islamic jurisprudence, ethnicity, and class, for example. In effect, the secular government sees halal as an expression of dispersed claims or requirements among diverse Muslim groups. In all this, Malays constitute a group of modern Muslim consumers with a particular history and geography of halal. Even halal understandings and practices of Malays who are relatively relaxed must be seen on the backdrop of the way in which halal has been standardized in the Malaysian context. Most of all perhaps, halal among Malays in London exposes a whole range of ambiguities involved in the tension between religion and the secular in everyday life. One such ambiguity is the important question of halal certification that I will now turn to.

Chapter 4

The Other Side of the Logo[1]

In a study of the potential halal market in the United Kingdom, the Malaysia External Trade Development Corporation (MATRADE) writes that the labeling of halal products is "of course crucial for its acceptance by the UK Muslim population" (http://edms.matrade.gov.my/domdoc /Reports.nsf/svReport/86763F1A9777C47A482571010012E74B /$File/PMS-%20Halal_1.doc?OpenElement), and that the majority of the U.K. Muslim community is "quite liberal and receptive" in their acceptance of the halal logo from countries such as Malaysia. However, Muslims in the United Kingdom are aware that "bogus" halal certification exists. Typically, this is done by writing halal in Arabic on signs and shop facades. MATRADE advises Malaysian manufacturers to "liaise" or "coordinate" with "reputable" authorities such as Halal Food Authority (HFA) or Halal Monitoring Committee (HMC). What is more,

> the non-existence of a recognised single body to oversee the certification of halal is an added advantage for Malaysian certified halal products, especially if Malaysia is successful in promoting the MS 1500 [the standard prescribing guidelines for production, preparation, handling, and storage of halal] as an international standard. The acceptance amongst UK Muslim consumers of the JAKIM [the Islamic Development Department of Malaysia] halal logo is also added advantage to the promotion of Malaysian halal products in the UK.

This chapter argues that the proliferation of halal in a multitude of commoditized forms is premised on complex understandings and practices of certification. I begin by exploring how my informants understand and practice divergent forms of halal certification and logos in London and, second, discuss these findings from a more theoretical perspective. To my knowledge, there exists no systematic anthropological exploration of halal certification so far.

The title of this chapter, "The Other Side of the Logo," indicates a point subject to empirical substantiation. Although more and more types of halal certification, and thus logos on halal products, are appearing in the halal market in London, in the eyes of many Muslim consumers, this marking tells them relatively little about the actual or intrinsic "halalness" of the product. The concept of frontier is important in this respect, that is, the "halal frontier" understood as a "frontier of knowledge" indicates that a better understanding of halal materiality is required. More specifically, I will investigate "cultivated" or "civilized" surfaces of halal commodities against their intrinsic or inner "wilderness"—the other side of the logo as it were.

The (secular) Malaysian state has successfully become the authoritative body with the power to certify halal, and this has important implications among middle-class Malays on the frontier. What is more, halal evokes national and patriotic sentiments as well as ways in which Malay ethnicity is tied to the Malaysian state.

Before examining certification below, I briefly discuss ways in which institutions may generate authority among individuals in everyday life. Institutions can gain legitimacy by a certain kind of "grounding in nature and reason," and these institutions (halal certifiers) try to instill in consumers "a set of analogies with which to explore the world and with which to justify the naturalness and reasonableness of the instituted rules" (Douglas 1986: 113). With reference to Durkheim, Douglas (1986: 113) argues that an institution "must secure the social edifice by sacralising the principles of justice. This is Durkheim's doctrine of the sacred. All the other controls exerted by institutions are invisible, but not the sacred." For Durkheim, the sacred is invoked explicitly, and halal marking can be seen as an institutional attempt to sacralize commodities in a religious market. Douglas (1986: 113) writes that "the sacred flashes out from salient points to defend all the classifications and theories that uphold the institutions." Marking some commodities as halal sacralizes some commodities against others and invokes the (religious) authority of certifying institutions.

In my discussions of halal with the *imam*, Mascud, in London, the question of proper halal certification and logos on commodities frequently emerged. Mascud argues that, in Britain, most types of halal certification are quite unreliable, because producers, traders, and certifying bodies do not really understand the definition of halal and proper certification. Mascud further maintains that because the state has no authority to carry out inspections in Britain, the unregulated market is open to fraud. Conversely, he trusts JAKIM's state certification of halal and its distinctive logo.

To use halal labels or logos on products, a certifier must inspect all related enterprises and organizations. This certifier "guarantees that the enterprise respects a set of predetermined criteria. Any label supposes inspection of the technical process and/or the management methods" (Daviron and Ponte 2005: 42). Hence, the halal certification of products thus provides a way of branding that takes place at two concurrent levels, that is, in the sphere of institutional relations and in the sphere of material objects. In both these spheres, branding concentrates on "techniques of packaging, positioning and promotion which together serve to reshuffle constantly the separate and linked relations among and between institutions and commodities" (Moeran 1996: 279). The certification of halal products and marking them with logos are essential in Muslim consumption, because the "halalness" of products is not easily verifiable: smell, texture, or taste cannot determine whether a product is halal or not.

In my survey, I asked 100 Malay respondents about halal certification. Virtually all these Malay respondents are familiar with JAKIM state certification, and most of them prefer it for various reasons. Respondents also indicate that, after state certification, certifiers such as the HFA and HMC are reliable and trustworthy. Conversely, they consider certifiers such as Islamic Food and Nutrition Council of America (IFANCA) (www.ifanca.org) and the Central Islamic Committee of Thailand relatively reliable, but consider local certification by an *imam* or food expert unreliable. In summary, Malaysian state certification by JAKIM is preferred to other competing forms of halal certification in this rapidly expanding market.

My survey findings largely correspond to those of Ahmed (2008: 658) on halal meat in London, that is, Muslim consumers mainly prefer to use local butchers and convenience stores. Moreover, only 16 percent of customers ask about authenticity in halal butchers and convenience stores. To my knowledge, there are no Malay-run butchers in London. Contrary to my Malay respondents and informants, who were aware of halal in supermarkets, Ahmed's respondents did not really know about this alternative. Ahmed summarizes his findings as follows:

> Muslim consumers make decisions based on more than one element, that is, price, and loyalty to and trust in local butchers. The majority of Muslims do not trust supermarkets in spite of visible certification/logos—authenticity is the most important factor over availability, price and quality. (2008: 664)

Conversely, my Malay informants, who are accustomed to shopping for halal in supermarkets and hypermarkets in urban Malaysia with visible state certification, in general trust standardized halal certification in London.

The huge Tesco Extra hypermarket in Slough outside London boasts of having the widest "world foods" and Asian world foods ranges including halal in Britain. Downstairs there is a more traditional halal butcher operating as a concession selling fresh meat. In November 2006 in Tesco Extra, I found Maggi chili sauce produced and certified in Malaysia, and a halal "Curry Special" butter chicken with no certification/logo on it.

In August 2009, I found the following certified halal products in this same store: Malaysian Lingham's chili sauce and a range of similar products from Malaysia. In 2009, the logo representing Malaysian state certification was now more "national," that is, it did not state that JAKIM was responsible for certification but instead Malaysia as a country; Koka Oriental Style Instant Noodles produced in Singapore and certified by Majlis Ugama Islam Singapura or the Islamic Religious Council of Singapore; Mae Ploy Green Curry Paste produced in Thailand and certified by the Islamic Committee Office of Thailand; Knorr Mushroom and Chicken Flavored Soup Mix produced in India and certified by IFANCA, one of the world's major certification bodies; Great Food Falafel produced in the United Kingdom and certified by HFA (this product was also kosher certified by two different Jewish certification bodies) (figure 4.1); Tahira Turkey Nuggets produced in the United Kingdom and certified by World Islamic Foundation, a U.K.-based certifying body (figure 4.2); and Chicken Pakora produced in the United Kingdom by Gazebo and certified by HFA.

In that same store, I found the following uncertified halal products: Chicken Goujons produced in the United Kingdom by Aisha's Original Recipe; Chicken Spring Rolls produced in the United Kingdom by Maysum; Chicken Korma and Pilau Rice produced in the United Kingdom by Mumtaz; Easy Chef Doner Kebabs produced

Figure 4.1 Great Food Falafel produced in the United Kingdom and certified by HFA as well as kosher certified by two different Jewish certification bodies

Figure 4.2 Tahira Turkey Nuggets produced in the United Kingdom and certified by World Islamic Foundation

in the United Kingdom; Maggi/Nestlé Coconut Milk Powder Mix produced in Sri Lanka; Strawberry Jelly Crystals produced by Ahmed Foods in Pakistan; and Achar Gosht Curry Mix produced by Shan in Pakistan.

This development testifies to the proliferation of halal as a globalized religious market. It also shows that Southeast Asian countries such as Malaysia, Thailand, and Singapore dominate halal certification followed by IFANCA and local certifying bodies in the United Kingdom, whereas the Middle East and South Asia are not really involved in institutionalized certification by Islamic organizations or state bodies. The dominance of these Southeast Asian countries also reflects another important point for my London ethnography, namely, that it is in Southeast Asia that halal most of all extends into food other than meat and even into nonfood products. Hence, as most smaller halal shops and butcheries in London are run by Muslims that are not of Southeast Asian descent, it is most common to find halal meat as the primary commodity here, whereas the halal products found in a Tesco hypermarket, discussed above, are more rare.

"Anyone Could Have Put Up That Halal Sign"

The empirical material suggests two registers of understanding and practice of halal certification among Malays in London. The first group is relatively strict or purist about halal certification, whereas the second group tends toward a more pragmatic approach to these contested questions. Selected informants in each group represent diverse approaches to halal certification. In other words, these informants are exemplars of the scale of strategies involved in everyday halal consumption.

The heading to this section, a quotation from Nazli, illustrates the sentiments toward halal certification among the first group of informants. When we discussed the state of halal certification in London, Nazli complained that, as a general tendency, shops and butchers' shops simply put up a sign displaying the word "halal" in Arabic and/or English. In the eyes of these Muslims, marking such products and premises lacks proper certification by a trustworthy certifying body that can be held accountable for the "halalness" of products. Nazli also argues that anyone could put up a sign in Arabic that indicates halal: "I worry about local halal certification sometimes because you can see people we don't even know creating their own halal signs and putting them up." Conversely, Nazli finds that halal certification by HMC or HFA, the two main certifying bodies in Britain, is more reliable and trustworthy. As we saw in the previous chapter, he acknowledges that halal in the United Kingdom and elsewhere is increasingly about politics, power, and business—and not so much about religious beliefs and injunctions. Nazli hopes to see more shops and restaurants selling "properly" certified halal products; as long as the certification process is ensured by a dependable certifier, he does not take the trouble to look at labels that could reveal if products contain alcohol or gelatin. To Nazli, proper halal certification with a convincing logo is sufficient proof that the products are fit for Muslim consumption.

As in the case of most other informants, Nazli patronizes a local halal butcher's shop for meat; this requires trust in the Muslim butcher because, in most cases, there is no visible certification in such facilities. Many Malay consumers in London favor local halal butchers, because the meat is affordable compared with halal meat in supermarkets. Conversely, halal in supermarkets is normally certified by HFA, HMC, or another Islamic organization. Consequently, to consumers, the proper "branding" of halal commodities may represent a luxury that is not always affordable. Modern consumers are accustomed to a wide range of logos on products. Unlike halal meat in butchers' shops, halal products in supermarkets are packaged, so customers can look for recognizable and proper logos on packaging among the expanding world food ranges. To most informants, asking about certification in a halal butcher's shop in London means questioning the authority of the butchers. Most of my informants share this reluctance to enquire about certification and thus question the authority of halal butchers even though they are well aware that fraud occurs frequently.

Fatimah looks for two things when buying food in London: proper halal certification by a reliable certifier or "vegetarian food," even though she is not a vegetarian. None of my respondents or informants are vegetarians, despite the fact that becoming a vegetarian would solve many problems for Muslims who are fastidious about halal certification. I shall return to this point in Chapter 6. Fatimah only accepts certification by a local *imam* or food expert if this person is familiar to her. Thus, she often uses websites as consumer guides for halal in London:

> I usually refer to the London Central Mosque website. Because when I came to London to study it was on this website I learned about where to get halal food. So, if I'm familiar with a local Mosque or Imam I trust it's halal.

This sentiment shows that trust and personal relationships are essential in the understanding and practice of halal certification. Normally, however, Fatimah would go to Green Valley supermarket, a delicatessen, because she feels that it sells halal meat certified by trustworthy authorities, the meat is fresh, and in general the quality standard is high. What is more, this supermarket has a range of ethnic specialties from the Middle East, for example.

Alina, for one, is outraged that, in London, she can find false halal signs in Arabic that pretended to represent proper certification. Alina describes this as "private" or "shop" certification. As we saw above, Alina linked Malay fastidiousness about halal to the *Shafi'i* school of jurisprudence. With regard to the everyday understanding and practice of halal certification in London, she tends to see other groups of Muslims as "others," whether they are very pragmatic, individualistic, and relaxed ("bad Malays" as it were) about their religion or very strict and dogmatic. Similarly, for instance, several informants see Brunei and Bruneians as being extremely purist about halal. Thus, when certification is an important question for one's own shopping for halal, it can also become an important marker of ethnicity and gender distinctions, for example.

When discussing halal with Hasan, the issue of thrift dominates:

> On weekends I go to Tescos. On weekdays, normally I buy halal food in a halal butcher shop near my place and I go to Lidl because it's cheap. They also have halal meat in Lidl, but in terms of certification I'm not so sure about this meat. I have never seen a logo. That is why I go to the proper halal butcher shop in Asda, for example. I think they have a HFA logo stamped on it.

The price level of properly certified halal conditions a range of shopping practices in everyday life. Hasan explains that, as a Malay in London, he is used to the reliability of Malaysian state certification, and that all other types of certification would be second to that. As a consequence, halal certification and logos are important for everyday shopping, during which he compares these types of certification with the unachievable state standards.

Zurina is aware that, although McDonald's and Kentucky Fried Chicken are not halal certified, more and more proper alternatives for Muslims in London are emerging. She reasons:

> The thing in London is that McDonald's and Kentucky Fried Chicken are not halal, so if I like to go to a halal fastfood place I go to the Chicken Cottage or any other fastfood place that is halal-certified, halal logos at their doors.

Zurina had chosen Chicken Cottage after checking on the Internet and noticing the halal logo on the façade of a Chicken Cottage outlet. In general, she acknowledges all the authorities "as long as it is a body, a well-known and big organization that has undergone certain processes of the law." When I was out shopping for halal with Zurina and her flatmate in halal butchers' shops near their home in south London one day, I noticed that logos of certification were rare and not overtly displayed in these outlets. Zurina reasons that even though she feels that enquiring about certification in some of the butchers' shops is embarrassing, she would do it anyway, as many of these establishments simply put a sign on the door when they do not have a certificate. In other butcher shops, the certificate is put up so far away Zurina cannot see whether it is HFA or another body. The point here is that proper halal is conditioned by visible certification, as a logo that inscribes institutional relations into material objects. Hence, the surface of these products represents a frontier surface that can be "civilized" by proper certification.

In other smaller stores catering for a Muslim audience in Zurina's neighborhood in south London, halal meat is the primary commodity, whereas it is more difficult to find halal-certified nonmeat products. This point draws attention to the fact that certification of nonhalal food to a large extent is a Southeast Asian trend. During my fieldwork, I found the most halal-certified nonmeat products in large supermarkets as we saw it above, in the Chinese supermarket Wing Yip, and in Chinese stores in London's Chinatown. These products were either certified by authorities in Malaysia, Thailand, or Singapore. These halal nonmeat products were hard to come by in smaller shops in Edgware Road or Whitechapel Road, for instance, that in most cases are run by Middle Eastern of South Asian Muslims.

The last informants in this register are Usmirah and Henny, who are flatmates. When I discussed halal with these two women in a café near University College where they studied, it was clear that they are uncertain about the state of halal certification in London. In fact, when Usmirah and Henny go about their daily shopping, they explore the labeling of products for any haram substances such as alcohol or gelatin. They scrutinize the ingredients of halal-certified products as well, because they perceive that the certifying bodies in Britain lack credibility and authority and are only involved in certification for financial gain. As Usmirah notes, "We look at logos, signs, labeling, ingredients, and then we decide. It's just that we are more familiar with the JAKIM logo." Because Usmirah and Henny often look at labels on food, they are not really familiar with the wide range of halal logos in the London market.

This group of middle-class Malays is relatively strict about the halal/haram binary that requires proper certification. They are often interested in the certification of not only meat but also a whole range of other products. In this way, they support the current proliferation of halal. Furthermore, among this register of modern Muslim consumers, halal is not an individualized choice in everyday life but a religious injunction that should inspire a particular form of Muslim lifestyle.

"In Our Belief If Someone Says It's Halal, We Just Take It"

The heading to this section is a quotation from Binsar that transpired during our discussion of halal in a Malaysian halal restaurant in Edgware Road. Compared with the more purist Malays in the first group, Binsar and the other Malay informants in this second group are more pragmatic and relaxed about their understanding and practice of halal certification. As an expression of this type of sentiment, Binsar explains to me that basically he trusts producers and sellers to live up to halal requirements, and that it is not his responsibility as a Muslim consumer to mistrust their intentions. Pragmatically, he also argues that there are no significant differences between various types of certification, such as JAKIM and local certification in London: "I would take both, JAKIM and local certification in London, there's not too much of a difference anyway." Binsar trusts the signs in Arabic stating that a product, in a butcher's shop or restaurant, is halal. He concludes that "in our belief if someone says it's halal, we just take it. So if anything is wrong, we just blame the producer or trader." To Binsar, certification by an *imam* or food expert would be at the "bottom of the list," but he "wouldn't say I wouldn't take it."

Binsar's friend Abdul who is also present in the Malaysian halal restaurant in Edgware Road this evening reflects similar sentiments. Abdul puts it plainly that, in terms of halal and halal certification in London, "I'm just not too concerned. I couldn't be bothered, I am a bit ignorant, so if I see a halal sign I wouldn't do more research." Abdul is involved with United Malays National Organisation (UMNO) work in London but is not aware of Malaysia International Halal Showcase (MIHAS), and the state halal vision seems to be relatively insignificant and distant in his everyday life with his wife and children in north London. As we saw it in the previous chapter, he feels that "when you live outside Malaysia and can't really get what you need you just have to shut one eye." Some of my informants indicate that everyday pragmatism in many cases becomes the order of the day when living abroad and without the imagined safety of state-certified products. Moreover, this informant pinpoints a feeling present with a number of my informants—the multiplicity and ambiguity involved in everyday halal consumption:

> I actually find it a bit confusing when I see halal products such as bis-cuits and sardines. I am sure that there are different interpretations in our religion, but the way that I have been taught at school is that halal only applies to meat. So these new products are confusing.

However, Abdul recognizes that the Malaysian state discourse on halal overwhelmingly is about business and profit and not to the same extent Islamic devotion: "There is a lot of profit to be made on halal. Personally, I'm more liberal about eating non-halal, but the market is still very untapped. Even if I'm not very strict I would support halal as business." As one of the few informants, he indirectly critiques the massive commercialization of Islam that figures so prominently in the state discourse as well as the halal hype in London. As a consequence, financial or patriotic support for Malaysia through halal consump-tion becomes the driving force behind practice rather than halal as an expression of personal religious devotion.

My study shows that although halal is important as an identity marker for all informants, it also requires a constant and shifting engagement of many Muslim consumers. At the same time, trust in halal is inseparable from visible certification and logos by some kind of trustworthy authority, be it a halal butcher who embodies this authority and trust or packaging with logos on them in a convenience store, supermarket, or hypermarket.

Unlike these young Malay men, Kamaruddin, who has been liv-ing outside Malaysia for a longer period of time, has not been widely exposed to Malaysian state halal certification. Kamaruddin is the only informant not familiar with Malaysian state certification, which had not been institutionalized at the time he left Malaysia. In terms of halal reliability, Kamaruddin prefers local authorities such as HFA or HMC. More pragmatically inclined informants such as Kamaruddin simply trust the authority of these butchers' shops, which for the most part are not certified by any organization. Kamaruddin made clear to me that "there are times when you don't know whether it's halal or not so you just say a Muslim prayer before you eat." He describes himself as a "flexible Muslim" who is not overly subjected to religious injunctions, as was clearly demonstrated by his attitude toward halal and halal certification. I could not help speculate that in the eyes of some *dakwah* Malays, Kamaruddin could be considered a "bad Malay."

While Alina and Hasan are fastidious about proper halal certification in London, another Malay couple, Murni and Altaf, are more pragmatic. I first met Murni and Altaf at Malaysia Day Carnival, and the points below transpired during a discussion of halal in a Starbucks outlet in Edgware Road. Murni admits that the couple is not very particular in terms of halal. They are only particular about pork. However, Murni and Altaf are concerned when buying gifts for visiting other people's places: "Then we do pay particular attention to it and go to a supermarket and select proper halal certification." This point reflects the social significance of halal certification among some Muslim groups and individuals.

As we saw above, when asked why some Muslims are more fastidious about the understanding of halal and its practice, most informants indicate that a preoccupation with halal depends on the forceful impact of schooling, and thus the state, which provided information about halal as part of the Malaysian education system. As might be expected, halal knowledge and practice is also generated within families. Although most informants are equally exposed to this type of knowledge in the Malaysian school system, everybody also acknowledges that individuals and groups have divergent understandings and practices of halal. Therefore, bringing food to other people's homes or as gifts is a sensitive issue, and the best thing to do, as a Muslim, is to ensure that what they bring is as properly certified as possible, as in the case of Murni and Altaf.

With regard to the couple's personal halal food consumption, they are fairly pragmatic, although for nonfood products such as shoes, Altaf contends that she will never, for example, buy a pair of shoes without enquiring whether they are made out of pigskin. She emphasizes that Muslims cannot touch pigs, and if they do, they have to wash in a certain way. Thus, Altaf would prefer more certification of leather products. Despite the fact that consumers see themselves as relaxed with regard to halal food, they may be more fastidious about nonfood products that are not traditionally part of halal.

This second group of Malay consumers either reluctantly accepts the importance of halal and its certification or simply rejects it as a material, and therefore shallow, display of belief that is unnecessary in their everyday lives. However, the understanding and practice of halal among these more pragmatic Muslims cannot be separated from the fact that halal production, trade, and consumption are undergoing drastic changes, and that halal is part of powerful discourses and practices globally.

I will now first sum up my findings and then discuss these findings from a more theoretical perspective. This empirical exploration of halal demonstrates that proper certification is a question that even the most pragmatic Muslims are aware of and must negotiate in their everyday lives. In my discussion, I have not included other ethnic or Muslim groups, because this research effort is based mainly on Malays who embody a particular trajectory of halal. However, research I have done with other Muslim groups, such as Pakistanis, Bangladeshis, and Indians, suggests that, between and within these groups, purism and pragmatism represent powerful distinctions. In other words, distinctions between the self and the other are often manifested in being fastidious versus relaxed about halal and its certification as a moral register or category. Informants explained to me that visible halal certification and logos on products is probably the most reliable marker of halalness that Muslim consumers can observe in their everyday consumption.

Informants preferred state-certified products by far if they were readily available. State-certified halal in Malaysia was described as "familiar," "trustworthy," "reliable," and "convincing." The way in which halal has developed in a country such as Malaysia will probably affect future tendencies in the global halal market with particular respect to certification and standardization. Thus, the Malay Muslim consumers can be seen as representative of trends that may prove significant in this global religious market.

My survey data showed that virtually all respondents were familiar with and preferred state certification and its logo. To my mind, the power concentrated with the state in the form of symbolic capital to bureaucratize, standardize, and certify ideas and practices of halal may be the ultimate state effect, so that the modern state is materializing out of "the powerful, apparently, metaphysical effect of practices" (Mitchell 1999: 89). This allegiance to the state is preconditioned on trust in its capability to certify and authenticate proper Islamic consumption.

However, the current lack of availability of these products necessitated a pragmatic approach to the consumption of halal in everyday life. Certification by local halal bodies such as HFA or HMC, marginally linked to the secular state in Britain, was also acceptable, whereas local halal certification by an *imam* or food expert was considered unacceptable.

Pragmatically, most informants simply trust the authority of halal butchers or convenience stores that for the most part are not certified by any organization. When I was out shopping for halal meat with middle-class Malays in these butcher shops, in most cases, there was no visible or recognizable certification. Malay consumers tend to feel embarrassed by enquiring about certification because it may question the authority of the butcher. These Malays were well aware that because there was no actual state authority involved in this type of halal consumption, the butcher shop was not really accountable for the halalness of the meat. As a Muslim consumer, when doubting whether a product is halal or not, there are at least two alternatives. One strategy is vegetarian food, and another is kosher food. Second, as Kamaruddin discussed in plain words above, one can say a Muslim prayer before one eats. This point reflects another aspect of the transformation of halal. Several informants explain that it is legitimate for Muslims to consume *mashbooh* or even haram food and drink if halal is not available. As the current halal market expands and transforms, however, it becomes increasingly difficult to disregard or bend halal requirements.

Unlike Chinese Muslims in China, who kept away from non-Muslim foreign franchises such as Kentucky Fried Chicken (Gillette 2000: 121), for most of my informants, everyday pragmatism is the order

of the day when living abroad and without the imagined safety of
state-certified products. In fact, most of my informants would visit a
Kentucky Fried Chicken outlet in London, but some would be more
concerned about the food there than others.

This form of pragmatism was obvious in the fieldwork when I
accompanied Malays going (halal) shopping in London—thrift, convenience, and trust in local butchers and shops were keywords that
shaped everyday halal consumption. Thrift is important, as many of
these Malays are students who have to be economical when spending.
Local halal butchers were favorites with many Malay consumers in
London because the meat here was affordable compared with halal
meat in supermarkets. However, the meat in these halal butcher shops
was often seen to lack proper certification. Conversely, halal in supermarkets was normally certified by HFA, HMC, or another Islamic
organization. Consequently, to consumers, the proper "branding" of
halal commodities can become a luxury that was not always affordable. However, in the eyes of many Muslims, it is unclear how certain
types of products and certification processes may affect price levels.

These middle-class Malays work hard to navigate the complex
halal market meaningfully to determine whether a product can be
trusted or not. In a wider perspective, my empirical data suggest that
the majority of respondents and informants are dissatisfied with the
labeling of products, that is, these Malays and other Muslim groups
advocate for more specific information on labels about potentially
haram or *mashbooh* substances such as gelatin or alcohol.

Certification by a "trustworthy" religious authority is essential, and familiarity with halal certifiers often increases consumers'
trust in such halal certification. However, the relationship between
availability, certification procedures, and price shape halal shopping
practices in everyday life. Different Muslim groups understand and
practice halal differently from other ethnic and Muslim groups in
the marketplace and often perceive other groups as overly pragmatic
or purist about halal. Moreover, the length of stay in Britain plays a
significant role in patterns of halal consumption. Malays in London
tend to be more relaxed about halal, the longer they have lived outside
Malaysia. In general, women appear more focused on halal compared
with men.

Some of my informants indicate that halal in Britain is being over commercialized, and that this has led to unhealthy competition and fragmentation among Muslims. There is a fine line between increased focus on halal certification among consumers, producers, and certifiers and what is seen as excessive commercialization emptying halal of its "religious" contents.

Trust in halal certification is essential, and this type of religious consumption evokes some old anthropological discussions. An example of such a question is that for traders, there is not unlimited freedom to make gains at others' expense, that is, traders are accepted only as long as their fairness in business is confirmed by their standing as honorable persons. This point is salient in the halal market. As we shall see in the subsequent chapter, a halal butcher wearing gold can be seen to be excessive and thus incapable of possessing proper halal understanding and practice. Consequently, generating too much wealth on halal should ideally be balanced by some measure of appropriate social/religious aims for the benefit of the Muslim community. Supermarkets such as Tesco and Asda have introduced a halal chocolate bar (www.ummahfoods.com). Among other slogans, it is advertised as "community & chocolate close to your heart? Isn't it time your chocolate bar did something more than just taste good?" Furthermore, the print on the chocolate bar says that "10% of net Profit goes to Charity." Interestingly, I could not identify any certifier of this product. While halal in Malaysia expands to cover more and more products that are either state certified or certified by Islamic organizations recognized by the state, new halal products in Britain are in many cases not properly certified in the eyes of some Muslim consumers.

The (secular) Malaysian state has successfully become the authoritative body with the power to certify halal, and this has important implications among middle-class Malays on the frontier where a plethora of certifiers are claiming authority. The Malaysian state is in many ways unique in delocalizing halal commodities and ideas on a global scale, and it is against this backdrop the ethnography should be seen. However, the authority of the Malaysian state applies to more than halal in a strict sense. Halal also evokes national (in Malaysia and in London, there are no serious competing Malay attempts to challenge the authority of Malaysian state certification) and patriotic sentiments as well as ways in which Malay ethnicity is tied to the Malaysian state. All of this seems to meet in bureaucratically certi- fied halal by the ethnicized state, and it fuels visions and efforts to develop and control the halal market as an economic and religious/ political strategy. State-certified halal can be evoked as a form of shopping for the state (Fischer 2008a), that is, the transformation of more traditional and symbolic types of reverence for authority in the form of Islam, royalty, and Malayness in Malaysia. Instead, the state now demands the patriotic consumption of subjects in return for various forms of responsiveness, most clearly through delivering economic growth and spending power. In other words, the economic transformation of Islam in Malaysia has displaced Islam as a source of traditional legitimacy.

The exchange of certified halal commodities illustrates the argu- ment that every transaction is necessarily a "social strategy" (Sahlins 1972: 303). Sahlins (1972: 313) writes that "the economic flexibility of the system depends on the social structure of the trade relation." In the market for halal, there exists a particular trade relation. Consumers buy commodities that ideally comply with certain religious standards, and the trader not only profits but also claims a measure of authority. Marking or tacking commodities with logos helps to personalize this form of exchange or transaction, that is, ideally the producer, trader, and consumer all share the symbolic content of the halal logo.

"Business...is always personal at one level and impersonal at another," Hart (2005: 5) writes. We always, he argues, experience society as personal and impersonal at once, and the halal market evokes the point that "business and market relations more generally have a personal and social component" (Hart 2005: 28). Going to a local halal butcher, for example, may embody such a personal and social component. However, this form of business is regularly seen by some of my informants to lack the more "impersonal" and thus abstract form of organizational control and inspection involved in Malaysian state certification, for example. One informant called this personal, inexpensive, and questionable form of certification "shop certification" as an expression of lawlessness on the halal frontier. Conversely, halal in supermarkets is mainly seen to be not only imper- sonal but also reliable and expensive.

Advertising can contain religious and totemic (sacred images that transcend totems and emerge through collective interpretation and representations) dimensions that bring out its culturally potent force (Sheffield 2006: 3). The case of halal certification lends itself well to an understanding of religious aspects of advertising. By branding halal objects as commodity totems, advertising empowers Muslim consumers to belong to a particular group (Sheffield 2006: 27). Hence, advertising certified halal products, and marking them with logos, is essential to Muslim consumption because the "halalness" of products is not easily verifiable as smell, texture, and taste cannot determine whether a product is halal or not.

This is a form of "logo logic" that works by attaching political and moral messages to lifestyle brands and communicating these branded messages (Bennett and Lagos 2007: 194). In general, systems of certification have grown considerably, but the diversity of these systems often confuses consumers (Bennett and Lagos 2007: 204) as we have seen above. At the same time, the coordination of certification can be problematic because of the absence of institutional support—states and governments tend to be reluctant to regulate different certification and standards systems (Bennett and Lagos 2007: 204). When institutional support is not in place,

> the viability of many systems depends on finding the resources to pay for the monitoring and certification of corporate compliance, and expand markets for certified goods so that companies may eventually self-regulate on grounds it is simply good for business. (Bennett and Lagos 2007: 194)

Consequently, "companies often initially prefer those systems that demand the least, which weakens the strength of subsequent signaling to consumers" (Bennett and Lagos 2007: 204). In other words, halal certification at times tells consumers little about "the other side of logos." There is a distinct element of political economy present in the way in which halal certification in complex ways links the different levels of the social scale such as individual consumption, the marketplace, Islamic organizations, and the state.

Chapter 5

Urban Halal Landscapes[1]

This chapter is an exploration of the spaces or landscapes in which middle-class Malays in London consume halal. Halal and halal certification, discussed in the previous chapter, have much to do with the context in which halal is displayed and sold: it is not just a matter of "halalness" as an intrinsic quality that complies with a particular religious injunction. I analyze the proliferation of halal in London as an urban form of space making or landscaping. As halal is delocalized and globalized as a religious market, it moves frontiers and contributes to new forms of space making. Thus, halal is being lifted out of its base in halal butcher shops into public space, advertisements, and hypermarkets. Although Muslim space making in general has been explored in a growing body of literature (Gottreich 2007; O'Meara 2007), the spatial contexts of producing, displaying, selling, and shopping for halal have received modest attention. The central argument is that shopping for halal cannot be divorced from the context in which it is practiced. Hence, the spatial context of food consumption as practice may be just as significant as the intrinsic qualities of the food and its ingredients. Halal is shaped not only by aesthetics and religious self-understanding but also by much more mundane understandings and practices. I show that halal spaces such as restaurants, halal butcher's shops, grocery and convenience stores, supermarkets, and hypermarkets figure prominently in Malay narratives that effect particular forms of understandings and practices of modern halal consumption.

In itself a city such as London can be said to be a charismatic entity (Hansen and Verkaaik 2009: 5). The authors use the term "charisma" "liberally" and extend it to "larger, and non-human, entities such as cities, sites, objects and collectivities" (Hansen and Verkaaik 2009: 6). Charisma is today being democratized in the marketplace, for example, and this has "entailed a measure of objectification—standardization, definition and tangibility—and a commercial exchangeability of objects, attributes and skills that are assumed to produce charisma" (Hansen and Verkaaik 2009: 7). The proliferation of halal is a good example of a particular type of urban exchangeability that is imbricated in the mundane practices of everyday shopping to effect charisma among Muslims.

Food constitutes a particular object domain (Miller 2000: 117), that is, these commodities embody their own specificities and uniqueness (Miller 2000: 106). I argue that halal food works "in a continual interaction mediated by the specific form of industrial commerce through which the material manifestations of this relationship is continually being recreated" (Miller 2000: 122). Everyday understandings and practices of halal hinge on a constant balancing of notions of intrinsic (and powerful) properties of commodities that can be bracketed, negated, or amplified by the context of handling, style, and display.

The book *Halal Food: A Guide to Good Eating—London* (Azmi 2003b) by the Malaysian publisher KasehDia reviews over a hundred restaurants, takeaway counters, and cafés in London. Much more than strictly traditional halal requirements are involved in guiding Muslim consumers: the spatial context (atmosphere/feel/ambience) of food consumption as practice may be just as significant as the intrinsic qualities of the food and its ingredients. The various establishments are classified according to their halalness, for example, whether alcohol is sold or food is produced/served by Muslims/non-Muslims. During my fieldwork, "spatial trajectories" (de Certeau 1984: 115), that is, stories that traverse and organize places and link them together, were prominent in halal narratives. I explore how my informants understand and practice these often ambiguous halal spaces and offer a "sense" of these divergent spaces around London. What is more, I discuss articulations of difference between "eating out" and "eating in" in the lives of middle-class Malays. By "eating in" I mean shopping for halal meat and other types of food in London to cook these in informants' homes.

Muslim space making or landscaping is the production of "the 'social space' of networks and identities created as individuals interact in new contexts, as well as the production of the 'cultural space' that emerges in a wide variety of ways as Muslims interact with one another and with the larger community" (Metcalf 1996: 2). The proliferation of halal is contributing to social and cultural space making in London. Often it is certain activities, shopping and eating, for example, that contribute to the creation of "Muslim space" (Metcalf 1996: 6). A central theme in this chapter is the display and transmission of the Arabic word "halal," written in Arabic and/or Roman characters, and its involvement in the production, recognition, and contestation of halal space in London, that is, how the increased focus on the proper marking of halal space, and not urban theories and theorists' work on how space is produced, effects certain practices in the everyday lives of my informants.[2] Turkish migrants in Germany, for example, take great care to prevent the moral contamination from haram (unlawful or forbidden) meat that can seem threatening to them in Germany. These concerns have moved to the forefront in the diaspora, whereas these dietary laws are "nearly unconscious" in Turkey (Mandel 1996: 151). The question is how middle-class Malays as an aesthetic community with a particular and conscious trajectory of halal understand and practice urban halal spaces.

A Malaysian National Halal Cuisine

A large part of my fieldwork took place in halal restaurants, particularly Malaysian ones. It was in these restaurants I ate halal food and discussed halal with Malay key informants, restaurant owners, and halal traders. At the end of this section, I discuss the food served in these restaurants. Several of the most popular Malaysian restaurants in London advertise themselves as "Malaysian (halal) cuisine" on signs. I understand a "cuisine" to be a set of classifications performed by a given culture and the rules associated with them: "both those which regulate the combination of elements thus defined and, more

generally, those which govern the whole set of practices and representations connected with the production, gathering, preparation, attri-
bution and consumption of food" (Fischler 1988: 286).

In my conversations with Hamza, the owner of a Malaysian halal
restaurant located in a basement in Edgware Road, many of the central themes of this chapter come out. During my frequent visits to this
restaurant, it was obvious that customers comprised non-Muslims as
well as a diversity of Muslim groups. This point fits well with the fact
that the location of the restaurant was Edgware Road, which has a
particular Muslim "sense" to it, that is, most of the shops, kiosks,
restaurants, cafés, money transfer agencies, barbers, and estate agencies surrounding the restaurant were businesses with Muslim ethnic
backgrounds.

Hamza stresses that halal is also about lifestyle and ethos and not
only a question about a religious injunction pertaining to food and its
intrinsic qualities. To Hamza, one of the main motives for starting a
restaurant specializing in "authentic" Malaysian halal food is that this
cuisine is well known among the Islamic community in London. Even
more importantly, alcohol is not sold in the restaurant. However, as a
guest you are allowed to bring your own alcoholic drink, but I never
noticed any guests doing so. In the eyes of Hamza, his restaurant is
"100 percent halal" meaning that not only is the food in itself halal,
but alcohol is not sold in this establishment, and income is never used
for any haram activities such as gambling, for example.

Yet another motivation for running the restaurant is to demonstrate to non-Muslims that Malay waitresses (Hamza only employed
Malays) who would be wearing a *tudung* (a long headscarf) are accommodating, modern, and efficient Muslim women. Hamza's vision is
to serve Malaysian halal cuisine for Muslims as well as non-Muslims
in an atmosphere of "cosmopolitanism," as he puts it. This cosmopolitan sentiment evokes a form of powerful "national cosmopolitanism"
in Malaysia as a particular local strategy "to negotiate and absorb new
transnational or other universal experiences." The state accommo-
dates and encourages transnational exchanges with a specific focus on
trade and finance (Yao 2003: 222–223). So transnationalization and
global capitalism are "something localized in shaping national aspirations and industrial aims" (Yao 2003: 223). The vision to globalize

Malaysian halal is a good example of a Malaysian "national cosmopolitanism" at work in a diasporic context as a "politics of cosmopolitanism" (Pollock et al. 2002: 12).

Hamza states in plain words that trust is essential in the halal market in London, and he relies not only on trustworthy, but also on more expensive, suppliers of halal meat. In the eyes of Hamza as well as my informants, distinctions between halal/*mashbooh*/haram are to a large extent premised on context and practices. Hamza, for example, rumors that when in London, some Malaysian ministers and even the prime minister would visit a Malaysian restaurant even though a non-Muslim Chinese Malaysian ran the restaurant. Many Malays, including most of my informants, consider non-Muslims unqualified to prepare and handle halal food. The thought of the Malay political elite visiting such a restaurant seems odd in the eyes of Hamza when the Malaysian state simultaneously tries to promote halal on a global scale. In both state discourses and with Malays more generally, halal should ideally be produced and handled by Muslims. What is more, this restaurant has a bar, and alcohol is served, and thus, income is also considered as coming from a haram source.

Hamza tries to represent the wealth of food in multiethnic Malaysia, all halal, however, in the restaurant's menu. The basic ingredients were imported from Malaysia to achieve "authentic" Malaysian taste.

My informants who often frequent Malaysian restaurants in London consider these dishes quintessentially Malaysian "national" as opposed to fish and chips or roasts, for example, which are seen to be typical British food.

In Hamza's restaurant, there are several tourist posters from Malaysia but no visible Islamic paraphernalia such as plaques with Islamic calligraphy. The atmosphere clearly indicates that this is a "Malaysian" restaurant; it has a particular Malay(sian) feel to it comparable with what you could find in urban Malaysia. During fieldwork in 2006, this restaurant hosted a *Hari Raya* celebration, which signifies the end of the fasting season of Ramadan, and throughout the day, a large number of mainly Malays enjoyed the free food and hospitality of the restaurant (figure 5.1). On this day, *nasi himpit* (compressed rice cubes), *rendang daging* (rich coconut beef), and *sayur lodeh* (curried vegetable stew) were served among other festive dishes.

Figure 5.1 Open house *Hari Raya* celebration

Another Malaysian restaurant in north London likewise advertises itself as "Malaysian halal cuisine" (figure 5.2).

This restaurant is part of a food court located in Oriental City Shopping Mall in Colindale, a suburban area of north London. Adjacent to the food court is an Asian supermarket that also sells fresh halal meat and a whole range of other halal products. This supermarket is designed to accommodate the tastes of various Asian groups that live in the area, that is, signs clearly mark sections and isles as "Korean," "Indian," and "Japanese," for example. Halal products include Malaysian ones such as Lingham's chili sauces. On Lingham's website (http://www.lingham.com/aboutus.htm), it is stated that all the company's products are halal. Another Malaysian halal-certified product in this supermarket is canned mackerel in tomato sauce produced by Ayam Brand in Malaysia. This product is also fully halal certified: "All Ayam Brand products are Halal certified by reputable Islamic authorities. It is indicated on the label by a Halal logo" (http://www.ayambrand.com/__More _information/halal-certified-food.html) (figure 5.3). These products are stored next to the refrigerated counter containing halal meat.

Figure 5.2   Malaysian halal cuisine

The owner of this restaurant, Siti, contends that over the past 15 years, because of Islamic revivalism and increased political awareness of the commercial aspects of halal in Malaysia, political leadership has equated Malaysian "national" food with halal. This transformation is significant not only for Malays but also for Chinese and Indians. This

Figure 5.3 Ayam Brand mackerel in tomato sauce

point was substantiated during fieldwork in Malaysian restaurants in London, as many Malaysian Indians and Chinese in particular frequent these restaurants. In this restaurant in north London, a plaque with Islamic calligraphy is visible behind the counter. This restaurant is famous for its *nasi goreng kampung* (a type of fried rice flavored with pounded fried fish). In Bahasa Malaysia, *kampung* means "village," and for many Malaysians, the *kampung* signifies romantic ideas of national authenticity. A significant number of Malays in Malaysia still live in *kampungs*, and many urban Malays go back to the *kampung* of their relatives during holidays and religious festivals.

Another Malaysian halal restaurant is discreetly located in a basement in fashionable Paddington, west London. In this mall eatery, plaques with Islamic calligraphy as well as the Malaysian national flag call attention to the focus on a Malaysian halal cuisine. This affordable restaurant, which especially attracts students, is popular with both Malaysians and other groups, and it was crowded throughout the day. The atmosphere is relaxed, like a café, and smoking is allowed.

Another popular halal eatery among Malays in London is the canteen in Malaysia Hall that houses one of the most prominent Malaysian students' associations, the Malaysian Students Department for the United Kingdom and Eire. One of my informants, Kamaruddin, confides to me when we were having lunch there one day that he considers Malaysia Hall a very "political" space in which the presence of the Malaysian state and Malaysian Islamic doctrine is excessive. In many ways, this place reminds Kamaruddin of some of the more dogmatic aspects of Malaysian revivalist Islam he left in the 1970s. Typical dishes were *nasi lemak* (rice soaked in coconut cream) and a variety of curries.

In these eateries, most Malay women wear the *tudung*, but by no means all. Based on my periods of fieldwork in urban Malaysia, it was clear that comparatively more women would be wearing the *tudung* in the Malaysian setting. This point indicates that claims for piety and Islamic identities through Islamic dress for women in particular are not necessarily stronger in a diasporic context. Indeed, the diasporic context can be supportive of more relaxed sentiments compared with the homeland.

The menus in these restaurants included a wide variety of dishes, a few of these already mentioned above. Often these dishes formed part of a set menu, that is, an affordable and fixed menu indicating that the customer has either no choice or limited choice of menu. My experience was that set meals always included meat dishes. Typical dishes served in these restaurants were *nasi lemak* (rice soaked in coconut cream); varieties of *nasi goreng* (fried rice); *nasi kandar* (rice served with other dishes of curry with chicken, fish, beef, or mutton and often together with vegetables); *rendang daging* (rich coconut beef); *ayam percik* (grilled chicken dipped in rich coconut gravy and spices); *biryani* (a mixture of spices, basmati rice, meat/vegetables, and yogurt); *mee mamak* (fried eggs and noodles); *asam laksa* (rice noodles served in a fish, vegetables, and spices soup); and *laksa lemak* (laksa served in a rich coconut gravy). Malaysian national cuisine in these restaurants is heavily influenced by the country's multiethnic composition. In all restaurants, *teh tarik* (literally, "pulled tea") (hot tea made from black tea and condensed milk whose name comes from the pouring process of "pulling" the drink during preparation) was on the menu.

The vision to forge a Malaysian halal cuisine has fused with the way in which the state has institutionalized and regulated halal in Malaysia. The dual focus on halal and a Malaysian national cuisine seems to come together in the spaces of the Malaysian halal restaurants discussed above. London boasts an extreme number of ethnic restaurants, cafés, and takeaways, but it was only some of the Malaysian restaurants that branded themselves as Malaysian halal cuisine. However, many restaurants in London serving Malaysian food are not halal certified.

In a broader perspective, there has been an increasing articulation of regional and ethnic cuisines (Appadurai 1988), and Malaysia is an example of how halal can add to this trend. The critical features of national cuisines "are the twin processes of regional and ethnic specialization, on the one hand, and the development of overarching, crosscutting national cuisines on the other" (Appadurai 1988: 22). Appadurai explores the emergence of a national cuisine in India from the 1970s onward through cookbooks.

A similar development of a Malaysian national cuisine can be traced to the publication of classic cookbooks such as *Cook Malaysian* (Lee Sook Ching 2006), first published in 1980. The Malaysian Chinese author includes recipes for a long range of traditional and modern Malay (no mention of halal) and Chinese dishes. The author recognizes some important trends that have changed since this book was first published, namely that "people are now more health-conscious.

Obesity, diabetes, heart conditions and many other health problems are very common and people now realise that we are in control of our health, and we are 'what we eat'" (Lee Sook Ching 2006: 10). This point reflects the way in which health and eating have become national concerns that target oil, salt, and food enhancers, for example (Lee Sook Ching 2006: 10), as problematic and as central to personal and group identities. Cookbooks such as this one have been formative of national cuisines in India, Malaysia, and elsewhere. In Malaysia, this trend was paralleled by the growth of Islamic revivalism, on the one hand, and the growth of a large urban Malay middle class, on the other hand, who was the primary audience for cookbooks such as this one. What is more, the emergence and consolidation of national food is tightly linked to diasporic culture among migrant groups (Wilk 2002: 80).

The forging of a Malaysian national cuisine has fused with aspirations for Malaysia to become a world leader in halal. In fact, on November 4, 2006, the BBC (http://news.bbc.co.uk/2/hi/asia-pacific/6116878.stm), under the heading "Malaysia Dishes Out to Raise Profile," announced that the Malaysian government is trying to "raise the country's international profile" and offer businessmen cash incentives to open "thousands" of Malaysian restaurants worldwide:

> According to the Malaysian government, which clearly keeps a close eye on such things, there are just 376 Malaysian restaurants to feed the six billion people who live outside the country. So its government has set a target of raising that number to 8,000 by 2015.

These visions evoke the point that national cuisines are constructed in the interfaces between nationalist projects and cosmopolitanisms as well as global expectations in that "countries are nations and are expected to have things national, including a cuisine. International migrations, tourism and the associated travel and food writing are among the important factors generating these demands" (Zubaida 1994: 44).

Ideally, Malaysia's "name will be more renowned globally," the BBC reported. This ideal is inseparable from the wider halal vision, as halal has become a form of standardized national cuisine for Muslims and non-Muslims in Malaysia. However, when I discussed the Malaysian state's vision to "globalize" a Malaysian (halal) cuisine with Jeti, the woman Malay entrepreneur discussed above, Jeti complains that the current Malaysian political leadership is not "capitalistic" enough for this vision to be fulfilled. The point here is that these restaurants are also political spaces or contexts for halal.

A major challenge for the vision to globalize a form of Malaysian halal cuisine comes from the dominance of Thai ethnic cuisine. Thailand successfully set up a Halal Science Center in 2003 at the country's largest university, Chulalongkorn University, and has created its own national procedure for halal certification (www.halal-science.org). Thailand has made a major advance in the halal market, as it has a globally recognized ethnic cuisine and is a world-renowned tourist destination, and ingredients for Thai cooking are widely available. Among Malays in London, it is a widely held notion that the Thai government has subsidized restaurants around the world. Unsurprisingly, in London, you can find a vast number of Thai food spaces that by far exceed those of their Malaysian counterparts.

The Malaysian trade commissioner with the Malaysia External Trade Development Corporation's (MATRADE) London office explains to me that this subsidizing and "financial assistance" is taking place "subtly" and "not openly." In the eyes of the trade commissioner, it is unfair that Thai food mainly consisting of "a few popular dishes like Tom Yam and Green Curry" should put Malaysian food in the shade, especially considering that Malaysian food is far more diverse, due to the multiethnic composition of the Malaysian population. To illustrate this point, *New Straits Times* on May 11, 2006, reported that the chairman of the World Halal Forum in Malaysia, an interest organization that tries to promote halal globally in the interfaces between the state and corporations, encourages "players" to catch up with competing countries such as Thailand that had "aggressively developed itself to reap profits from the lucrative sector." At the same time, the Malaysian vision to become a world leader in halal is intimately linked to a particular dimension of modern diasporas in urban spaces around the world, that is, an economic dimension linked to investment and trade.

My informants were regular guests in these restaurants, and they enjoy this kind of national halal food and the spaces in which it is prepared and served. The question I turn to now is how these Malays in London more generally understand and practice "eating out."

Eating Out

The Malay *imam*, Mascud, complains that it is unconvincing when restaurants in London advertise themselves as halal when in fact only the chicken, for example, probably is halal certified. In the eyes of Mascud, a restaurant that does not display a halal sign could not be considered a proper halal space. Only if a restaurant is clearly marked as halal in Arabic, it is a suitable halal space (figure 5.4).

As we saw earlier, he does not recognize a restaurant as halal if it sells alcohol, much in the same way that a pizzeria cannot claim to be halal if it uses and stores ham together with halal meat or allows the same utensils to be used uncritically for all types of food. He mentions that once a Bangladeshi member of his congregation invited him to his restaurant. This restaurant did not display a proper halal sign, as alcohol was sold to cater to non-Muslims. According to Mascud, this

Figure 5.4   The front door of a Malaysian halal restaurant

restaurant did not qualify as halal because income was coming from a haram source. Consequently, his favorite restaurant in London is an Afghan restaurant in which alcohol is not allowed under any circumstances. Mascud can be seen to represent an authoritative Malaysian state discourse on halal, and the question I now turn to is how my informants understand and practice these sentiments. I explore ways in which informants map the full range of practicing eating out in London and then plot themselves in. This discussion of space is in some instances inseparable from the previous chapter's exploration of certification.

Alina is not comfortable going to places such as Kentucky Fried Chicken and McDonald's because halal options are limited and so is the knowledge of what my informants consider the proper handling of halal. The design and menus in these outlets are comparable with what you would find in similar urban spaces around the world. Alina, similar to several other informants, states that it is tiresome, for example, to only be able to eat the Filet-O-Fish burger at McDonald's. As we have seen, in Malaysia, state bodies certify the entire menu at McDonald's and other similar fast food outlets, and thus, going there is quite unproblematic from a Malay's perspective. In all McDonald's outlets in Malaysia, Malaysian state halal logos are ubiquitously displayed on the façade of the restaurant as well as inside.

In London, Alina asks at restaurants if she is uncertain about the halalness of the food served. She has to ask because there is no general information available in these outlets. Alina feels that these enquiries are taken seriously in these eateries. She considers an entire restaurant space nonhalal because of particular nonhalal ingredients in the food, on the one hand, or the improper handling of the cutlery or wok, on the other. At the same time, she acknowledges that other Muslims would frequent such establishments because they are either unconcerned with halal or the craving for the food overshadows their doubts.

Zurina is aware that even though McDonald's and Kentucky Fried Chicken in London are not halal certified, more and more proper alternatives for Muslims in London are emerging. She would not go to a nonhalal restaurant such as Pizza Hut except for gatherings with non-Muslim friends because this was a time to show that you are a "flexible Muslim." In that instance, Zurina is extra careful to search for vegetarian food and drinks. In the restaurant Subway, for example, Zurina argues, the meat is nonhalal, but you can eat the tuna sandwich. However, friends had told her that the employees at Subway used the same gloves to prepare all different kinds of food, meaning that the food was *mashbooh* at best. Compared with this Malay register of halal consumption that is relatively fastidious about halal when eating out, another register is more relaxed and pragmatic about halal consumption.

For one, Irfan is flexible about going to nonhalal restaurants to eat, and if a non-Muslim restaurant is selling halal food as part of their otherwise nonhalal menu that is acceptable to him. What is more, Irfan is content about the provision of halal food in the hospital where he works. Other informants, however, complain that the provision of halal food in their workplaces or educational institutions is quite unsatisfactory.

Likewise, Murni and Altaf are fairly relaxed and pragmatic about halal in restaurants. For example, frequently Murni was traveling in connection with his work and then it was not always easy to find proper halal food. Consequently, Murni had to be flexible about his food choices, that is, he would eat a nonhalal beef burger in McDonald's. Altaf argues that in many cases, halal is most important when eating out with friends or parents, for example. If the parents notice that pork is being served in a Chinese restaurant, they will not accept eating in this particular place. Nazli refers to Chinese restaurants and takeaways in London that display a wide variety of halal signs. In Bayswater, for example, Nazli could identify several such Chinese establishments (figure 5.5). This restaurant sells a wide variety of Asian dishes. In principle, however, most informants would prefer to go to what they considered properly halal-certified places such as the chain restaurant Chicken Land (figure 5.6). On the façade of Chicken Land outlets halal in both Arabic and Roman characters marks this space as proper for Muslims. In terms of design, this type of establishment is comparable with a wide range of fast food outlets in urban Malaysia. The main difference is that in Malaysia such establishments all carry the Malaysian state halal logo outside as well as inside.

Figure 5.5 A Chinese restaurant in Bayswater

To sum up, the two registers of modern Malay halal consumption understand and practice eating out divergently. While the first register is fastidious about halal when eating out, the second register is more pragmatic about the practice of halal space. Informants within the more fastidious register of public halal consumption often evoke Western fast-food restaurants such as McDonald's, Kentucky Fried Chicken, or Subway (all fully halal certified in Malaysia) as problematic spaces that cannot be considered compatible with strict halal requirements. However, this register of Muslim consumers recognizes that in connection with socializing or work, for example, their halal requirements when eating out cannot fully be met.

Eating In

Part of the Malaysian halal vision is to see Malaysian shops in "global" places such as London selling all necessary products for cooking traditional Malaysian (halal) food. So far, this is just a vision, but one an entrepreneur such as Jeti, discussed above, is considering to address. Indian grocery stores around San Francisco, for example, generate

Figure 5.6 Chicken Land

"production and consumption of a range of texts, images, and commodities that participate in this ongoing construction of India and Indian culture" in a diasporic context (Mankekar 2004: 197). Malays in London do not have the opportunity to partake in this form of diasporic national culture when shopping for groceries to cook at home in London.

Before entering into how middle-class Malays in London navigate the halal landscapes of butchers, convenience, or grocery stores as well as supermarkets/hypermarkets, I discuss these in their own rights. Halal is highly visible in signs and logos in the urban landscape. There are hundreds of halal butchers in London, that is, shops that mainly sell meat. First, these butchers can be classified according to ethnicity. Some butchers are run by Pakistani, Indian, Bangladeshi, Mediterranean (figure 5.7), or Afro-Caribbean (figure 5.8) Muslims, for example. As discussed above, the ethnicity of the owners/butchers did not in any significant way condition the everyday halal choices of middle-class Malays. Another classification of halal butchers pertains to certification. Only a fragment of the numerous halal butchers in London are certified by the Halal Monitoring Committee (HMC) or the Halal Food Authority (HFA), the two major certifying bodies in Britain. The East End butcher in the picture is an exception (figure 5.9).

Much of the halal meat sold in London comes from convenience stores or grocery stores that also sell a wide variety of groceries

Figure 5.7   A Mediterranean grocery store that sells halal meat

Figure 5.8   A grocery store selling Afro-Caribbean and Asian specialties

Figure 5.9   A halal butcher certified by Halal Monitoring Committee

Figure 5.10   A convenience store that also sells Islamic paraphernalia

and sometimes Islamic paraphernalia such as stickers, rugs, holiday cards, and plaques with Islamic calligraphy among other things (figure 5.10).

The huge Tesco Extra hypermarket in Slough outside London discussed in the previous chapter, boasts of having the widest "world foods" and Asian world foods ranges including halal in Britain. Slough is a borough about 30 kilometers west of London and a highly ethnically diverse local authority. What is more, Slough is known to house a variety of dedicated religious groups. During fieldwork, this ethnic diversity was clearly visible in the store. A large percentage of shoppers were of Asian origin. Hence, it is no coincidence that this huge hypermarket stocks a wide range of "world foods" and "ethnic foods." Space in Tesco outlets in London's more fashionable West End that house a lower percentage of Asian groups is not filled with "world" or "ethnic" foods to the same extent. Here, "upmarket" specialties and organic products dominate the shelves.

As we have already seen, downstairs in the Tesco Extra store in Slough there is a more traditional halal butcher operating as a concession selling fresh meat. Anecdotal evidence from my fieldwork in this area suggests that Tesco, by using this store in Slough as an entry into the halal market, has reduced sales among halal butchers in the surrounding area. Around the same time, in the Asda supermarket in north London, I found HFA-certified chilled chicken and mutton, in other words, also undercutting the prices of local butchers. This point testifies to the big-scale spatial transformations that are taking place in the global market for halal.

MATRADE writes about this Tesco in Slough that it is

> working together with the National Halal Food Group by opening a "National Halal" Centre in this store for fresh Halal meat and poultry from November 2005. This business venture is initiated due to the growing demand from the local Muslim community for Halal Meat and poultry and also Tesco responds to the needs of the local community. Tesco is set to carry an extensive range of halal products which could include non-food products as well. (http://edms.matrade.gov.my/domdoc/Reports.nsf/svReport/86763F1A9777C47A482571010012E74B/$File/PMS-%20Halal_1.doc?OpenElement)

Thus, MATRADE maps the potential of the U.K. halal food market according to the performance of outlets such as this Tesco Extra in Slough.

The question I will now turn to is how my Malay informants understand and practice "eating in," that is, how halal products such as meat and the public spaces in which they are bought are conceptualized. I take seriously the contention that identity and morality "begins (but sometimes also ends) at home" (Miller 2001: 140). Halal food consumption in homes is often, but not necessarily always, linked to external global transformations and events such as the proliferation of halal and food scares.

My survey data from London show that most Malays prefer to eat in compared with eating out. What is more, these survey data indicate that Malays in London mostly shop for groceries in either hypermarkets or supermarkets, as it is also the case in urban Malaysia (see Chapter 2 for a discussion of the pluralization of shopping choices in Malaysia). These Malays, however, most often buy halal products in local grocery stores or halal butcher's shops. These practices are different from those of the Malay middle class in Malaysia, who mostly shop for halal in supermarkets and hypermarkets. In my conversations with food authorities and Islamic groups, I learned that rumors of fraud and falsely certified halal meat are common. The halal market in London is fragmented and unregulated, and the question is how this point conditions Malays' everyday shopping for halal in various forms of halal spaces.

Mascud lives with his family in Cricklewood, north London. He would normally shop for halal in a grocery store near his house, as this is the most convenient place in terms of location, price, and quality. Often he would also go to the Shepherd's Bush Market, a historic market that caters to a variety of ethnic groups selling both nonfood and food items.

When shopping for halal, he pays particular attention to the hygiene of establishments. My impression during fieldwork was that most of these halal butcher shops actually seemed to be clean. He explains to me that it is not enough to make sure that meat, for instance, is properly slaughtered if it is treated in an unhygienic manner or if the earnings are used for haram purposes such as gambling. Mascud, like nearly all my informants, agrees that even though it is not an Islamic injunction that halal be produced, sold, or handled by Muslims, he prefers to shop for halal from Muslims.

The range of dishes my Malay informants would cook at home reflected a complex mix of Western and Asian food. In the eyes of most informants, a proper home-cooked meal consisted of meat (poultry, beef, or lamb mostly), rice, and vegetables. Hence, these elements were essential to their home cooking. Chicken and a variety of chicken curries in particular were favorites with my informants, that is, chicken was considered healthy and affordable at the same time. Meat was eaten on a daily basis and included in a variety of curry dishes as well as quintessentially "national" dishes such as *rendang daging* (rich coconut beef). Another favorite dish cooked at home was *nasi goreng* (fried rice). Informants would also cook seafood at home. The inclination toward Asian foods did not exclude Western dishes. For example, Zurina loved to invite her friends to an English-"style" breakfast that included halal sausage or roasted chicken. Interestingly, Western food is often considered "exotic" because of its "lack" of flavor compared with Asian cuisines of Malaysia and Thailand, for example.

These middle-class Malays are accustomed to a highly globalized, multiethnic, and cosmopolitan food market in urban Malaysia, and this is clearly reflected in their food choices when they "eat in." As long as the food is considered halal, they would cook a wide variety of dishes in their homes. Besides meat, which most of all is subjected to halal/haram judgments, alcohol and gelatin are often also sources of concern.

Another issue among some middle-class Malays in London is the limited availability of ingredients used in Malaysian cuisine. Often Malays will shop for these in Chinese supermarkets such as Loon Fung in Chinatown or elsewhere or Thai grocery stores. Some of these Malays bring back spices from Malaysia, or they ask friends and family to do so.

Many Muslim groups with divergent understandings and practices of halal compete in this expanding market in Britain and globally. However, my Malay informants do not prefer to buy halal from certain ethnic groups or avoid others. In other words, ethnicized space does not significantly condition halal consumption. Instead, as Mascud for one argues, appearance, piety, and devotion—being a "practicing Muslim"—are essential markers of trustworthiness when shopping for halal. Thus, the spatial context for shopping for halal conditions understanding and practice. For instance, if a butcher is wearing gold rings or necklaces, considered to be haram, Mascud reasons that the butcher is probably not sufficiently knowledgeable about halal either. However, as discussed above, Mascud represents a particular and authoritative halal discourse, and I will now explore how my informants went about shopping for halal in their everyday lives.

We saw above that Nazli was fastidious about proper certification. Consequently, halal space making hinges on certification above anything else. Like Nazli, most informants observe the atmosphere and appearance of the halal butcher or shop assistant to judge the halalness of the meat or other types of products. Local halal butchers were favorites among Malay consumers in London, because the meat is affordable compared with halal meat in supermarkets. Conversely, halal in supermarkets is normally certified by an Islamic organization.

Nazli contends that in London, most Malays would prefer to cook at home. As many of my informants are students like Nazli, it is obvious that the aspect of thrift, as Nazli notes, is central to Malay food consumption. However, even informants high in economic capital prefer to cook at home, and they feel that eating out is in many cases a pragmatic necessity in connection with a busy lifestyle of work and travels. Nazli acknowledges that eating at home was also a preference that was related to the familiarity of certain types of dishes such as chicken curry that could be personalized in the home. He even asserts that most Malays would try to find a house near a halal butcher or grocery store selling halal products. Data from my respondents and informants indicate that most Malays in London shop for halal because of thrift, convenience, and familiarity with a local shop rather than going to a supermarket or hypermarket as a primary preference. Informants would tell me that "best deals" are often discussed among Malays in London. When I was out shopping for halal with informants, we frequented butcher's shops that were said to have the "best deals" in halal meat.

In Murni and Altaf's local halal butcher's shop in Walthamstove, there are "extra services" compared with supermarkets. Still, informants are often not quite sure about halal meat at these butcher's shops, and they negotiate the affordable prices and high levels of service against the more expensive and reliable types of certification to be found in supermarkets. Comparing their local halal butcher's shop with Tesco, both Murni and Altaf would agree that Tesco is cleaner, and this is a point generally held by informants.

Unlike the majority of my informants, normally Fatimah shops for groceries in supermarkets such as Tesco Express (it was open 24 hours), Sainsbury's and Waitrose (a U.K. supermarket that is often considered upmarket) that is situated close to her home, and Green Valley (a delicatessen with a good halal selection and fresh meat certified by trustworthy authorities). Consequently, halal is to a large extent premised on the context in which it is displayed and sold and not simply halalness as an intrinsic and abstract quality that complies with a particular religious injunction.

Alina, who above was discussed as being fairly fastidious about eating out, is surprisingly relaxed about shopping for halal in butcher's shops and supermarkets in London. She uses Muslim websites (e.g., the website salaam.co.uk that features discussion forums, news updates, and a database on halal restaurants) to access information about halal and haram products, and she does not think that the current availability of halal products in London is satisfactory. However, above anything else, her shopping for halal is conditioned by thrift and convenience, meaning that local halal butcher's shops and grocery stores are Alina's favorites. Alina's husband, Hasan, does much of the couple's shopping for halal in halal butchers, convenience stores, supermarkets, and hypermarkets. Hasan finds the current availability of halal products in London satisfactory. To Hasan, the issue of thrift dominates, that is, he goes to Tesco on weekends because it sells not only clearly certified but also costly halal food, and on weekdays, he buys halal food in a halal butcher's shop near the couple's home or the supermarket Lidl because the price is low.

Like several other informants, Hasan's primary concern over halal in shops is cleanliness. Again, supermarkets are seen to be not only more hygienic but also more expensive. In the eyes of Hasan, it is comforting to see that in some halal butcher's shops, a copy of the Koran or a plaque with Islamic calligraphy is displayed, as this testifies to the devotion of the owner and employees.

Zurina discussed above, much like Alina, is surprisingly relaxed about shopping for halal in local butcher's shops compared with her understanding of halal restaurants. The central point here is that despite the fact that Zurina critiques many of these butchers for lacking proper or visible certification, the halal butcher's shops embody a certain "Islamic" authority and expertise Malays rarely question per se even if these customers are not quite sure about the halalness of products.

With reference to Claude Lévi-Strauss, it has been shown that the house as a social institution combines a number of opposing principles or social forms, thus reuniting and transcending incomparable principles adding to an appearance of unity (Carsten and Hugh-Jones 1995: 8). The house "transfixes" an unstable union, becoming "the objectification of a relation: the unstable relation of alliance which, as an institution, the house functions to solidify, if only in an illusory form" (Carsten and Hugh-Jones 1995: 24). The safety of this type of haven ensures that halal imports are emotionally accommodated and handled. Halal bought outside can become imbued with the values of kinship and unity associated with the house and above all with the kitchen. These kitchens of informants were comparable with those of the Malay middle class in Malaysia discussed above, that is, they were modern and equipped with kitchen appliances that helped inhabitants going about everyday cooking. My informants consume a wide variety of Western and Asian types of food available in London. Compared with Malaysia, where halal has become a kind of a naturalized standard, in London, middle-class Malays, as an aesthetic and moral community, are more careful about the halalness of food. None of my informants (except Kamaruddin) lived alone, and rituals of sharing in privacy seemingly purified and legitimized the understanding of otherwise doubtful halal practices in the complex and ambiguous halal market. In other words, the import of halal into homes may translate ambiguous or malevolent (uncertified or improperly certified) commodities into something benevolent that can be shared and enjoyed within families or with friends or flatmates. When meat in particular becomes a mere ingredient among others in a range of well-known and craved dishes and cuisines cooked at home, its potential malevolence is mitigated.

To sum up, most informants would agree that over the past few years, halal availability has improved greatly in Britain and London in particular. However, many Muslim consumers are uncertain about the moral implications of an expanding halal market and the pluralization of shopping choices and, thus, spaces, involved in halal. Even the most relaxed middle-class Malays in London experience confusion as halal spreads into new types of commodities and marks spaces in supermarkets, hypermarkets, and advertising. Belief, piety, quality, certification, cleanliness, thrift, patriotism, and convenience were all keywords to describe everyday shopping for halal among Malays in London. Ultimately, the contradictory responses of informants underscore a central theme, that is, halal certification authorized by the Malaysian state as well as other authorities does not necessarily inspire confidence outside one's own kitchen. Contradiction and ambivalence are to a large extent generated by the sentiment that outside the control of one's home, there are few clear answers. Thus, consumers often have to figure things out for themselves and work out everyday shopping strategies.

An increased demand for halal in London emerges in the inter-faces between discursive practices and political and economic forces, and these "actively create the material and imaginary landscapes of the city" (Jacobs 1996: 9). In turn, these trends contribute to ways in which "transnational Islam creates and implies the existence and legitimacy of a global public space of normative reference and debate" (Bowen 2004: 879).

I have shown that spatial trajectories are essential in Malay under-standings and practices of halal in London. At the same time, the vision to forge a Malaysian halal cuisine is an attempt to "national-ize" halal as a particular form of consumption, and this is also visible in London. Halal is now part of a huge and expanding globalized market, and this effects new forms of Muslim space making and landscapes. This transformation and proliferation of halal pluralizes everyday shopping choices in terms of stores and availability, and this is comparable with transformations among middle-class Malays in urban Malaysia. One major difference, however, is that it is only recently that halal has proliferated in London to create what con-sumers consider proper halal landscapes as contexts for everyday con-sumption. These halal landscapes are also important for Malays as an aesthetic community that is intertwined with a moral community. At the same time, the visible world, halal landscapes, is part of a more spiritual universe. Comparatively, eating out was seen by the majority of my informants to be more complex and problematic than eating in. Despite the fact that the halal market is complex and fragmented in London, informants were often pragmatic and relaxed about shop-ping for halal not only in butcher's shops in particular but also in supermarkets and hypermarkets. The conceptualization of halal com-modities to a large extent hinges on the context of their everyday handling rather than their intrinsic properties. When the halalness of products is not verifiable based on smell, texture, or taste, the context or space in which halal is prepared, stored, handled, or sold is "what you can see" as one informant told me. Informants would explain to me that cooking at home was mainly a question of thrift, but I con-tend that eating in, in the home, is also essential to the way in which halal is domesticated and purified among the Malays in London.

Chapter 6

Halal Sanitized[1]

This chapter deals with the sanitization of halal in the modern scientific world, that is, how Malays in London understand and practice halal (food) as part of modern discourses of meat/stunning, health/nutrition, food scares, science, heating/cooling binaries, and excess as well as kosher and vegetarian food. When informants evoke "science" below, this should not simply be seen as the flip side of Islam/religion. Islam in Malaysia and other parts of Southeast Asia more generally tends to be based on an inclination toward absorbing all styles of thought into one broad stream. This tradition is generally receptive to the argument that "Islamic doctrine and scientific discovery are really not conflicting but complementary forms of belief" (Geertz 1968: 106). For example, this is the case in several of the references and quotes below that originate in the Malaysian context and fuse discourses of health, spirituality, and Islam. This chapter ends with a discussion of the ethical underpinnings involved in modern forms of halal consumption and discourse. From being an Islamic injunction in the Koran, halal both evokes and is evoked by a whole range of discourses. In other words, this chapter captures how halal sits uneasily in and between a plethora of powerful scientific, religious, and political discourses that often overlap. Similarly, halal among the Durrani Pashtuns of Afghanistan has been explored as part of a Koranic domain that coexists with several other domains (Tapper and Tapper 1986). I take seriously Caplan's (1997: 30) call for investigating

the way in which people make sense of the huge varieties of information coming to them, especially about the relation between diet and health....Food, eating and diet are part of an arena of contestation and struggle not only over availability, quantity and quality, but also over meaning and representation.

It is to the question of meat I will turn first.

Meat and Stunning

My survey shows that among Malay respondents, it is meat most of all that is subjected to fastidiousness, that is, meat is the primary type of halal commodity despite the way in which halal proliferates into other types of products as well as services and handling. At the same time, the survey indicates that the vast majority of respondents, but by no means all, are against stunning. In my discussions concerning meat with informants, it was clear that meat is a natural part of proper and well-earned meals eaten on a daily basis. Meat appears to be endowed with both a positive image as prestigious and vital nutrition and simultaneously has a contrary image as dangerously immoral and potentially unhealthy. In the eyes of my Malay middle-class informants, meat is synonymous with "real" food eaten on a daily basis, but at the same time, it is mostly particular types of meat that are considered problematic with respect to halal.

Kitchens in Malay middle-class houses in Malaysia have been radically modernized and industrialized with the import of a multitude of kitchen appliances. Similarly, in London, modern kitchens and kitchen appliances are essential in the preparation of meat in particular. Hence, in a diasporic context, "authentic" or "traditional" ways of preparation seem to be overshadowed by modern forms of handling and preparation in an often rushed everyday life.

As halal proliferates in the material world and in discourse, it is increasingly difficult for informants such as Murni and Altaf, who consider themselves relatively "relaxed" about halal, to practice the "benefit of the doubt" with regard to halal. During our discussion in a café in Edgware Road, Altaf articulates this feeling in the following way: "As long as you don't know it's alright, but once the doubtfulness enters your mind, you are not supposed to eat any more." The logic here is that the powerful halal discourses that are commercial, religious, patriotic, and moral in nature demand that Muslim consumers cannot simply assume that their food is halal; certainty in the form of certification, for example, is required as a standard.

At the same time, meat shopping and eating is conditioned by more mundane considerations such as price, health, and taste. Many middle-class Malays consider chicken, for instance, affordable and healthy because it is "low in cholesterol" compared with "red meat." Some informants believe that meat is nutritionally important because it is high in protein. Informants would prefer fresh meat to frozen meat by far, and overwhelmingly, halal is associated with fresh and not frozen meat. Several of my informants would eat less meat in London compared with Malaysia because of the price level and halal anxieties. In this type of narrative, halal in London is seen as unreliable but not to such an extent that these Malays avoid eating meat to become vegetarians.

In Malaysia, the state halal discourse is clearly such that the stunning of animals prior to slaughter is unwanted. Informants who are against stunning argue that this sentiment is premised on "religion," that is, practicing the slaughter of animals in a certain way. In the eyes of these Malays, the stunning of animals by electrocution in a butcher's shop, for example, is appalling, whereas ritual slaughter without stunning ensures both the proper Islamic way and draining the blood, which removes bacteria that can cause diseases in humans. Some Muslims believe that the stunning of animals makes it impossible or difficult to drain the blood fully.

Other informants are not clear about the question of stunning. Ongoing discussions or studies on the subject have not convinced them to decide for or against stunning. These views are more likely to surface on the frontier as a border zone through which cultures interpenetrate in a dynamic manner, that is, this is not a discussion that surfaces normally in the Malaysian media, as stunning is a naturalized and nationalized halal practice.

Stunning is an important issue for Alina as for most of my informants, but she is puzzled by the variety of technical stunning methods, for example, electrocution. With regard to halal, the question of stunning proves to be highly controversial with religious demands, on the one hand, and animal rights groups, on the other. The *imam* Mascud makes clear that within Islam, scholars, groups, and organizations disagree about this issue. Slaughter in accordance with Islamic law has been permitted in the United Kingdom.

The Halal Monitoring Committee (HMC) is against the stunning of animals before slaughter, whereas the Halal Food Authority (HFA) accepts stunning. This point contributes to making these two organizations competitors with overlapping interests and claims for authority in the halal market in the United Kingdom. This study shows that meat is an essential type of food in the lives of my informants, but it is also meat that that is subjected to a range of sentiments and scares personal, national, and global in scope.

Is Halal (Food) Healthier?

Powerful discourses promote halal as healthy and pure in an age of food scares and uncertainty. In the book *Food and Technological Progress: An Islamic Perspective* by a Malaysian publisher, the authors make the case that with regard to halal, concerns about health and well-being are central to prohibition (Chawk and Ayan 2006: 74). Another book on halal published in Malaysia argues that "healthy nutrition means having a balanced diet, in order to maintain the balance that Allah has established in all matters" (Consumers Association of Penang 2006: 14). Running through much of this type of discourse is the notion that food is literally transformed and becomes part of human bodies (Lien 2004: 6).

In current attitudes to food, the ambiguities are that pleasures deriving from food are also the sources of anxieties linked to eating. These anxieties about appetite for food generate concerns about the moral fabric of society (Coveney 2000: xiii). Modern consumers are constantly subjected to warnings and admonitions often couched in terms of a scientific and calculated understanding of food in the field of nutrition (Coveney 2000: xiii). Hence, nutrition becomes "a technology of power...that produces new and ever more specific subjectivities for individuals and populations" (Coveney 2000: 104). However, "Positions of dissent around nutrition serve as reminders that discourses always intersect with, amplify and resist other discourses. As such, discourses open up ethical positions for subjects that may be both complementary and conflictual" (Coveney 2000: 106).

The question I address below is, first, how middle-class Malays articulate nutrition and health and, second, the extent to which halal understanding and practice relates to these wider issues.

All my informants were clear about what they consider healthy/unhealthy types of food, whereas the question of whether halal per se is healthier compared with nonhalal is far more contested and infused with ambiguity and uncertainty. Many informants, for example, are clear on the point that ritual slaughter and draining the blood makes meat healthier, and that this is backed by scientific evidence found on the Internet in particular.

Generally, in the eyes of informants, "healthy" food is that which is fresh and has just come out of the shop. Vegetables and fruit are always considered healthy, whereas junk food, "quick lunch," and "microwaved" food are seen to be artificial and unhealthy. What is more, too much fat, chemicals, oil, and sugar are not good for one's health. These sentiments closely follow state campaigns for increased health and against obesity in both Malaysia and Britain. Processed food in supermarkets is often considered unhealthy in a British context where food production is seen to be highly industrialized.

Several informants refer to arguments and "evidence" from various sources, mostly from the Internet, that pigs are more prone to carry a range of diseases and parasites. What is more, pigs are often associated with *najis* (filth). For most informants, pig avoidance makes your diet healthier, for example, you will avoid "bad" bacteria.

Unsurprisingly, perhaps, Mascud believes that halal is healthier. He lists the following reasons: the method of slaughtering, emphasizing that the animal should not be stunned and the draining of the blood removes diseases; halal is a religious injunction put in place by God; and halal is not open to human interpretation: "Maybe halal is healthy, but we don't know the real reason and take it as a test, a trial from God."

One register of middle-class Malays is convinced that halal is healthier. Arguments supporting this sentiment are that halal in the form of a food prohibition came into existence because draining the blood, for example, is healthy as it cleans out "germs." Such narratives tend to circle around health as one of the main reasons behind food taboos in Judaism and Islam, but these are being sanitized, that is, they are being subjected to demands for verification and substantiation that are not necessarily of a religious nature. Another narrative is that halal is healthier because it is a way of killing an animal that ensures that the meat is fresh.

The other register of Malays refers to sources claiming that halal is healthier, but these studies are not always convincing because they are seen to lack backing by proper scientific evidence. Thus, these middle-class Malays are skeptical about the source of these claims as well as their validity in the modern scientific world. However, some Malays believe that if an animal has not been slaughtered properly and the blood drained as fully as possible, the dried blood can actually "mutate" with human blood and cause diseases. Therefore, as Muslim dietary rules have assumed a new significance in the twentieth century, these Muslims strive to demonstrate how such rules conform to modern reason and the findings of scientific research. Henny, for example, explained to me that she was not entirely convinced about the claim that dried blood can mutate with human blood, but in general, she adhered to the idea that all the "reasons" in Islam could be backed by scientific evidence.

Informants who are unsure about the claim that halal is healthier often articulate that the quality of halal meat is good because it is "fresh" owing to the method of slaughtering. The freshness of food is idealized as something that is intrinsic to halal (avoidance of carrion), on the one hand, and freshness (healthy and traceable), on the other. For one, Irfan does not think halal is healthier, but he was told that the taste of halal meat is better because the blood has been drained. This point adds to the fact that often halal is seen as a kind of quality, "value added," or standard that relates to taste, smell, and texture. In general, informants are not capable of a direct comparison between halal and nonhalal, as they claim that they are not aware of having eaten nonhalal food.

When it comes to the question of whether halal is healthier, Abdul is unsure. Encouraging the researcher to look into the matter more closely he says that

> this is another perhaps interesting question for you that we would like to find out about because a lot of Muslims they believe in the goodness of halal meat from a religious point of view, but the scientific approach hasn't been covered. For example pork, we avoid it, we know

that Jewish people avoid it, but there are not many mainstream scientific opinions to say whether it is good or bad. I personally would like to know more about that. Some Imam says that if you do ritual slaughter the blood goes out, which is better for your health, but that is what the Imam says, we don't know. So I would like to hear more scientific explanations.

This call for a scientific substantiation of halal as a healthy alternative evokes the problem of religious institutions that claim authority in an expanding religious market, as we saw it in the case of certification. Even if some *imam* or *ustaz* (religious teacher) contends that halal is healthier, these claims must undergo some form of scientific verification. Hence, religious discourse and authority are not in themselves enough to convince skeptical Muslim consumers such as Abdul who tells me that he is quite "open-minded" about halal, but at the same time, he needs scientific evidence to be convinced about the relationship between halal and health.

To sum up, the issue of whether halal is healthier or not is contested among middle-class Malays. In most cases, the above discussions pertain to meat and not so much other commodities. Hence, my informants do not uncritically accept the powerful discourses that claim halal to be healthy and pure in an age of food scares, and it is to that aspect I will now turn. However, before doing so, I will take a quick look at organic consumption in the narratives of these informants.

In the United Kingdom and many other countries, there has clearly been a tremendous rise in the importance of green issues as part of public discourse (Miller 2001: 122). Most informants idealize green or organic products as healthy but acknowledge that they do not consistently buy these products because they are too expensive. Several informants had tried buying organic products, and this type of shopping was always associated with sophisticated taste and wealth. Even though organic halal meat and other types of products are emerging in the U.K. market, availability is limited, and middle-class Malays in general would not buy these products.

Islamic Food Scares

The powerful discourse on halal links this form of modern food taboo and food safety. An example of this is the excerpt from the book *Food and Technological Progress: An Islamic Perspective*:

> Obviously, the primary issue that is touched upon in the Muslim world
> with respect to food security is ensuring that the food supply is *halal*.
> Food is a sensitive issue in a Muslim community. As such, concern
> in ensuring that the food supply to a Muslim community is permis-
> sible from the eyes of Islamic *shariah* is justified. (Sallah and Sobrian
> 2006: X)

A chapter in the same book argues that with respect to food security from an "Islamic perspective," globalization together with the
advances in biotechnology increases the number of ethical questions
posed (Norwawi 2006: 8). Thus, with intensified trade and importa-
tion of food as well as nutritional and scientific knowledge, food is
becoming less and less "natural," "simple," and "traditional," and the
cultivation of food questions notions of nature and purity (Wallace
1998: 3). However, increased concerns over food security contradict
the fact that modern food in many ways is far more pure compared
with previous centuries (Burnett 1966: 279). Ironically, food safety
concerns have increased among the general public, the industry, and
the government. At the same time, food safety is always both a natural and a social process (Busch 2004: 171). Among middle-class families in London, for example, food scares such as Bovine Spongiform
Encephalopathy (BSE) "epitomise not only all that is wrong with
modern food production methods, but also mistrust of both government and scientists" (Caplan 2000: 199). The question I will now
address is to what extent the food scare discourses pertaining to meat
in particular condition the halal understanding and practices of my
informants.

All my informants were aware of food scares, especially in the
media in both Malaysia and Britain. Some informants acknowledge
that these food scares slightly affect their food consumption, that is,
mad cow disease and bird flu caused concern, but this does not in any
significant way change food habits. In fact, often middle-class Malays
are more concerned about the affordability of halal in London, which
makes them wonder about whether the meat has undergone proper
halal slaughter and certification. The relatively low price of halal in
butcher shops makes it unlikely that halal meat is "free range" that is
considered to be healthier.

For one, when we discussed this issue at Malaysia Hall, Nazli makes clear that Muslims believe that halal is essential because food becomes part of your body and it stays on. However, these concerns about food and body are largely unaffected by food scares in Malaysia and Britain, and they are not in any significant ways expressed through particular halal understandings and practice. In the eyes of Nazli, the reason for this is that Muslims consider salmonella, for example, to be dangerous mainly in a non-Muslim, Western, and industrialized production context. However, Nazli, along with most other informants, is not really conscious of the way in which the Malaysian state and government try to promote halal as pure in an age in which food scares are exposed locally, nationally, and globally on a daily basis. This point is backed by my survey, which showed that the vast majority of respondents were not consciously alert to the Malaysia International Halal Showcase (MIHAS) and the halal discourse in Malaysia. To sum up, all my informants were well aware about food scares, but this awareness did not in any systematic way change their (halal) food habits.

Science, E-numbers, and Genetically Modified (GM) Food

The more halal proliferates as a globalized religious market, the more "scientific" modes and methods of production and traceability become important for producers, traders, and consumers. The increased focus on such methods to verify commodities as halal based on "science" constantly expands the requirements to cover new types of commodities and practice, including cosmetics, pharmaceuticals, and hygiene products. Science in a variety of forms is a significant topic in the lives of my informants. A central question, for example, is why and to what extent informants avoid GM foods. My survey shows that among respondents, two equally large groups of modern Muslim consumers would avoid and/or buy GM food, respectively.

The central problem in much discourse about science and halal (food) is that, on the one hand, science is both seen as part of the solution to achieving more reliable and verifiable conditions for the production of halal and, on the other, science constantly modifies a range of food types that cannot be clearly understood as halal because of chemical reactions, for example, in the production process. Hence, these products are often seen to be "artificial" or "unnatural." This ambivalence is reflected in the narratives of my informants below.

Modern citizens as consumers in a "technological society" such as the United Kingdom expect and are expected to be informed and updated about "the possible consequences of eating fats, sugars or GM foods, and the advantages and disadvantages of different forms of exercise and diets" (Berry 2001: 4). The question is how halal fits into a whole range of modern scientific processes and discourses. "Technical sciences that we have allowed to proliferate may not be able to deliver the best moral rules we wish to live by," Tambiah (1990: 151) writes.

All my informants agree that in principle, a product cannot possibly be halal if it contains even extremely low quantities of questionable content, pig gelatin or alcohol, for example. In general, informants would agree that scientific methods and technologies are needed to ensure that production processes would live up to religious standards. Informants evoke "science" and "technology" to signify modern, controlled, and transparent processes of food production.

An important question in this respect is knowledge about E-numbers, that is, number codes for food additives that are usually found on food labels throughout the European Union. As an example, many informants are fastidious about E-47, a form of synthetic fat that can be of animal, and, thus, porcine, origin. Quite a lot of energy is put into finding, reading, and evaluating these E-numbers among Malays on the frontier. Even when halal products are certified with a visible logo, informants are not always sure about the certifiers' knowledge of or intentions in connection with halal. On the contrary, shopping was quite unproblematic in Malaysia where the state, at least symbolically and rhetorically, protects Muslim consumers by sanitizing halal in the interfaces between science and religion.

Abdul calls for more common sense in the idealization of science in halal. He feels that subjecting halal to ever increasing scientific modes of understanding and practice is a slippery slope that causes uncertainty. Thus, scientific standards based on moral and commercial interests condition everyday eating and shopping: "Where do you draw the line?" he asks during our meal in a Malaysian halal restaurant in Edgware Road and adds that idealizing halal at the "atomic" level is excessive, and that it displaces common sense as everyday guidance. Abdul is "aware" of the issue of GM food, but says, "I'm just not too concerned. I couldn't be bothered. I think in the future I would like to be more careful about this, but right now my priorities are more about work than health although I know it's bad." Several informants share this notion that halal is not or should not be a "scientific" question but rather something that should be "learned" or internalized as a form of cultural or religious knowledge.

Other informants do not think that common sense is sufficient to determine the halalness of a product with regard to E-numbers or extremely low quantities of doubtful contents. For example, Nazli relies more on a *fatwa* (ruling) of the European Council for Fatwa and Research, a private foundation of Islamic clerics and scholars based in Dublin. This organization issued a *fatwa* approving E-numbers, ingredients, and substances that may change form under production processes. He stresses that science in modern halal plays a major role for the purity and health of the body.

In the case of medication, Muslims can be more "flexible" informants agreed. If you cannot find halal in a given country, you are allowed to be flexible, but as discourse intensifies along with increasing availability in a country such as Britain, more and more focus is put on being fastidious. In this vein, Mascud during his four-year stay in London had pills prescribed, and he is concerned that these may contain doubtful gelatin. However, some Islamic scholars, he explains, argue that such medication does not necessarily have to be halal because it is not "original" but a highly industrialized product that serves a benevolent purpose. He agrees with most informants that science is important in halal, but that honesty in this market should be the moral driving force.

Some Malays in London admit that it has become more complex to determine the contents in products that are not meat-based, such as chocolate. The artificiality, particularly regarding GM food, of such products makes them "impure" and indeterminable, and some of my informants would try to avoid these products for health reasons. The food market has been delocalized, so that as a modern consumer in London you have an extreme variety of food available from many countries. This makes it possible to avoid GM food without missing any desired types of food. However, as a modern Muslim consumer you have to be skilled to navigate and practice this complex market, that is, look at labels, which show whether a product is GM or not.

When discussing the issue of halal and science with Murni and Altaf many of the above issues came together:

> *Murni*: You want information about gelatin, in biscuits, for example, but you have to know what to look for. Studies show that when meat is transformed into gelatin there is a change in the chemical elements and it is no longer identifiable with pork. Some say it's then all right and others that it's not.
>
> *Altaf*: We know that it's all right if it's fish gelatin in marshmallows, for example. E-numbers that derive from animals, people say you have to very careful about. My mom is very careful about that.
>
> *Murni*: Adding to that, my sister studied in Warwick for three years, and she goes through that process as well looking at E-numbers.
>
> *Altaf*: Her community is sort of very, very strict and you know there is a lot of information being circulated, consumer guides and the Internet. Sometimes they say that this or that company supports what's happening in Palestine or they would avoid other companies because there is a rumor that the food contains this animal product. They use information to avoid certain kinds of foods. There are also views around about being careful about utensils that have been in contact with pork. We are not very convinced about all that, we just try to avoid pork and buy ritually slaughtered meat.
>
> *Murni*: We had this conversation with our friends yesterday about that we don't really know where the meat comes from, halal butchers or Tesco. Our friends are very strict making sure that their food is good.
>
> *Altaf*: Actually, in the last few months there have been these issues about meat from Holland that was injected with pork.

These exchanges together with the previous discussions pinpoint a number of issues. The tendency among these middle-class Malays is that while meat is the primary type of commodity, the question of determining gelatin and other substances and how they may transform in an increasing range of products such as chocolate or biscuits is becoming more pertinent. Another issue is that fastidious informants develop skills to look for these substances in more and more products. Increased awareness among some Muslims stresses the need to situate your personal/group fastidiousness/flexibility in relation to the perceived understanding and practice of the other, for example, family members or friends. The narratives about halal and science above tend to circle around rumors or alleged "scientific" evidence circulated on the Internet in particular and thus in a variety of rumors that in general express fastidiousness about modern forms of halal. Few informants would openly, as we have seen, critique this heightened awareness.

Halal sits uneasily between discourses and practices of health, religion, and taste. Ironically, in much of this, on the one hand, science is both seen as part of the solution (traceability and control) to achieve more reliable and verifiable conditions for the production of halal and, on the other, science constantly modifies a range of food types that cannot clearly be understood as halal in the production process.[2] These discussions evoke the point that for modern consumers "nutrition" often works as both a scientific and a spiritual/ethical discipline in which the correct and proper ways of behaving in relation to eating figure prominently. Consequently, modern dietary and religious discourses are suffused with ethical and spiritual problems. Middle-class Malays in London are exposed to such discourses that attempt to discipline consumption and patrol and push the borders between taxonomical entities such as edible/inedible in a globalized religious market. The effects of these entangled discourses on everyday Malay Muslim consumption seem to be reinforced in a diasporic context. Although halal in Malaysia is ubiquitous in production, trade, and consumption, some informants find that halal is fragmented and unreliable in London, whereas others seem to enjoy escaping halal as a form of modern religious disciplining in Malaysia.

Heating and Cooling Food

The question I address in this section is to what extent humoral or medical systems of food classification interact with halal understanding and practice. There is a relatively large body of ethnographic studies of Malay eating habits in relation to systems of food classification. Ideas about "hot" and "cold" were introduced with trade and colonization in the region and in particular through Muslim traders and missionaries, who visited the Malay peninsula from around the seventh century. Moreover, Arabic medical texts elaborated Islamic humoral pathology, and thus, the concepts of hot and cold were

translated into Malay (Manderson 1986b: 127). Food is often classified according to its reputed effect on the body, that is, "a hot food
is so classified because it is said, in Malaysian English terminology,
to be 'heaty'; a cold food has a 'cooling' effect" (Manderson 1986b:
128). In the humoral system of classification, animal products, oily
and spicy foods, alcohol, and herbal preparations are hot, whereas
fruits and vegetables are cold (Manderson 1986b: 128). More generally, Malay food beliefs and taboos are ways of articulating "the
ascendance, or allowing for the control, of culture over nature"
(Manderson 1986b: 140).

In a fishing village on the east coast of the Malay peninsula, one
study found considerable variation in individuals' opinions about how
food items should be classified. However, there was broad agreement
that chicken, beef, goat, eggs, manioc, yeast, chili, and spices are hot,
and that fruits and vegetables are cold. Rice and fish were understood
to be neutral. The informants in this study would quite unproblematically combine the humoral knowledge and practices of traditional
healers and modern medicine (Wilson 1981: 391).

A study among Glaswegian Punjabi women demonstrated that
"they have been exposed to the medical orthodoxy of 'healthy eating'
and they also have access to the folk beliefs of their forebears from
the Indian subcontinent" (Bradby 1997: 213). These two models are
used in a complementary fashion to compensate for one another's
inadequacies.

Among my informants, it was only women who articulated
knowledge of the above humoral classification of food. However,
this knowledge was not directly related to the domain of halal.
Alina considers durian/rambutan (fruits that are most popular in
Southeast Asia) and grapes heating, and at home, her mother taught
her that eating too much of these fruits could be "dangerous" and
the next day she could be coughing. Fatimah would take tamarind
juice if ill because it would cool her body down. She tells me that
tamarind juice and ginger, for example, are "cultural" and "traditional" types of "natural" medicines in Malaysia that are also "quite
doubtful," that is, not everyone would agree to the reputed effects
of these types of food. For Usmirah, cucumber was quintessentially
cooling. Her mother had taught her about these classifications, but

she is only really conscious about them when together with her mother.

Only a few of my women informants are aware of and practice the above system of food classification. What is more, these ideas are not in any explicit manner related to halal understanding and practice. However, there seems to be one clear tendency flowing through informants' accounts when we discussed the composition and contents of a "proper" and "balanced" meal. All informants would agree that such a meal consists of halal meat, vegetables, and rice, which together can be said to represent both heating and cooling properties.

When Halal Is Excessive

As halal proliferates, an important question is when/if halal becomes excessive. In this section, I explore the extent to which halal can be considered excessive in the eyes of my informants. The majority of informants convey that halal fastidiousness/flexibility is a personal question. However, this articulation of individualized consumer choices emerges in the midst of often moralistic ideas and discourses about halal as a religious duty that is not open to interpretation or mitigation.

The book *Halal Haram: A Guide by Consumers Association of Penang* (2006) discussed above in many ways reflects the deepening and widening proliferation of halal that has been taking place in Malaysia. One effect of this is to expand halal into nonfood commodities such as crockery that allegedly can contain crushed bones from pigs.

Most informants found this proposition ridiculous, along with the ever-increasing focus on proper storage, transport, and handling. For one, Irfan supports these sentiments. However, the proliferation of halal into nonfood commodities also represents what Abdul referred to as an "untapped" and highly profitable market. This type of patriotic or national sentiment fits the powerful state and corporate discourses on halal. In other words, as long as there is a personal demand driven by religious devotion, halal is a lucrative business with opportunities Malaysia should not miss. Abdul wonders why there has not been any real debate about ways in which halal can be seen to become excessive or overly commercialized, effecting moralism and forms of Islamic materialism as a shallow display of religion that will tell you little about inner devotion.

Other Malays in London acknowledge that eating from crockery that could contain crushed bones from pigs actually was a real concern as was wearing pig leather. Alina, for one, agrees about these points relating to leather—leather from pigs is considered completely unacceptable, and if a Muslim touches this, he or she has to wash in a certain way. As halal is open to potential commercialization, some informants would appreciate it if leather were clearly marked with a type of logo. Often salespersons in shops cannot help in this respect. "There is a big market for clarity," as Alina explains. In effect, consumers should at least be made aware of what crockery contained and the origin of leather, or it should ideally be certified or labeled as halal if it lived up to a predefined standard. Much the same would go for handling, storage, and traceability that should receive much more focus.

Alina argues that in a way halal is boundless and could in principle expand into innumerable products and services, but she stresses that it is still the decision of the single consumer to desire or buy these products. Often informants would evoke the state-regulated halal market in Malaysia in opposition to London where many products are considered indeterminable. These ambiguities and doubts invite a desire for institutionalized halalness that is comparable with that of Malaysia. Mascud noticed the new chocolate bar from Ummah Foods that entered the market, and it was now one of his favorites. In his view, any product should ideally be halal unless otherwise stated, including crockery. Consequently, he suggests clearly labeling all haram products.

In general, these modern Muslim consumers face multiplicity and ambiguity when they try to understand and practice halal as proper or excessive. A couple of women informants gave details saying that even though they are not very fastidious about halal in hair shampoo and toiletries when shopping in Kuala Lumpur, they would definitely choose a halal-certified shampoo against one that was not halal certified. As one can expect, producers and traders in markets that have a sizeable population of Muslims are aware of this.[3] In a supermarket in urban Malaysia in May 2009, I found seven local and international brands of toothpaste that were all halal certified. In the same supermarket, I also found halal-certified vitamins and health products.

Alternative Strategies: Kosher and Vegetarian

Halal parallels the Jewish kosher,[4] which includes a number of additional prohibitions, for example, a number of marine species. Contrary to halal, kosher requirements have a longer history of systematic institutionalization, certification, and standardization. Kosher figures prominently in the narratives of my informants, who would quite unproblematically consume kosher. Only the *imam* Mascud would not consume kosher. He considers halal a religious duty for the *ummah*.

Some of my informants wonder why kosher is so widely available in the United Kingdom and globally when the number of Jews is relatively limited, whereas the halal market is only emerging in the new millennium. In the eyes of many Muslims in London, the Jewish system of kosher certification is seen as a model in the interfaces between religious revivalism, the state, and consumer culture.[5] The powerful discourses on halal envision that halal can develop vis-à-vis kosher but with a much larger global market base. Kosher compared with halal is often more costly because the production and certification processes are more elaborate than is the case with halal. Several informants find halal, in butcher shops, for instance, to be suspiciously inexpensive at times.

Informants would explain that if they could not find proper halal food, they would take "vegetarian" food, that is, avoid meat that is considered doubtful. "Meat eating and vegetarianism are two sides of the same coin—each being significant in opposition to the other" (Fiddes 1991: 4). A study of meat eating and vegetarianism in London demonstrated that vegetarianism and the model that positions meat eating and vegetarianism as oppositional should be reconsidered (Willets 1997: 111).

None of my informants were vegetarians, that is, they did not avoid meat eating for extended periods of time. Survey data stress this point. Hence, vegetarian/kosher food and fish constitute alternatives when halal is not available. Some informants would look for the

"V," meaning "Suitable for Vegetarians," sign on food in much the same way as looking for halal and kosher certification. "Suitable for Vegetarians" ideally indicates that no doubtful animal-based gelatin, for instance, is in the product. Many informants feel that vegetarianism is highly respected in the United Kingdom, so they are comfortable with the way in which vegetarianism is marked. However, only in 2006, the Food Standards Agency issued guidance on the labeling of foods as suitable for vegetarians. In this way, kosher and vegetarian food complements the everyday consumption of halal.

Halal between Gender and Generation

In general, women are more fastidious about halal than men. This point is supported by Gillette's (2000: 120) findings among Muslims in urban China. This sentiment is also reflected in my study. Alina, more generally, finds that within her generation, women, compared with men, are more focused on religion. The younger generation to which most of my informants belong have been more exposed to not only powerful halal discourses but also comparable discourses on health and nutrition. These discourses are often circulated in families but mostly within the educational system. With particular reference to halal, Mascud argues that

> when I was a kid Malays would still eat at the Chinese restaurant. But nowadays, it is very difficult, except for ignorant people. If somebody goes to a Chinese restaurant in Malaysia he is considered ignorant. In those days it was very rare to find a Muslim restaurant. Malay people they did not really get involved in business, but in agriculture and government. Now Muslims are very concerned and they are also involved in business such as halal.

This point reflects the relatively relaxed sentiments among previous generations of what Michael Peletz calls "ordinary Malays." Now halal is inseparable from the new generation of entrepreneurial middle-class Malays that is linked to the Malaysian state—global New Malays who are highly educated with a "we can" mentality compared with previous generations. All of this has heightened the awareness of taste, lifestyle, and religion of the younger generation of the middle class to which my informants belong.

Food has emerged as a highly political topic connecting individual bodies to abstract communities and techno-scientific innovations to moral concerns. At the same time, food systems are globalized to become entangled in complex webs of political and "national" significance, that is, ethnicity, Malaysia's vision to become the world leader in halal, aspirations to forge a national halal cuisine, and the growth of the Malay middle class in the interfaces between state and marketplace.

In many of the discussions above, there are explicit and implicit "national" narratives at play. Zurina's comment about enjoying English breakfast with halal sausages, for example, points to one important finding in this study, namely, that being fastidious about halal does not lead Malay individuals or groups in London to live secluded and extremely pious lives based on abstention in the diaspora. As we have seen, pragmatically, Malays in London negotiate proper halal understanding and practice in relation to the surrounding society and its transformations. At the same time, "science" and "technology" sit uneasily between middle-class Malays' halal understanding and practice on the frontier, that is, science is both seen as part of the solution and the problem.

To conclude, discourses of health/nutrition, religion, political visions, excess, patriotism, and business all meet in the proliferation of halal as an emerging religious market. In the everyday lives of middle-class Malays in London, the vision to globalize halal seemed distant and was often overshadowed by more mundane concerns. However, Malays in London directly or indirectly acknowledge that the global proliferation of halal is somehow connected to future prospects of a modern Malay Muslim diaspora emerging in the interfaces between Islam, the Malaysian state, and business. Some informants would complain about the unavailability of halal in their workplaces or educational institutions but never did this lead to social isolation or extreme fastidiousness. All of this is expressive of a modern Muslim diasporic group that adapts to and pragmatically reflects on everyday life in London. In other words, halal understanding and practice are not necessarily stressed in a diasporic context as many previous studies have indicated. For instance, a previous study of mine (Fischer 2008a: 184–87) demonstrated not only that Islamic banking[6] is widespread among middle-class Malays in urban Malaysia but also that this type of service tends to evoke ambiguity about a whole range of issues. None of my Malay informants in London use Islamic banking, and this fact supports my point that these Malays are relatively pragmatic about Islam in their everyday lives in London.

Links between halal and contemporary notions of science and health strongly evoke middle-class sophistication of Malays in London. My informants' consumption of halal communicates clearly about their knowledge and practices enabling them to identify legitimate, proper, aesthetic/moral, and healthy choices in a complex and expanding market.

Informants link science and halal in divergent ways. In the eyes of some informants, science/technology and halal per se are inseparable. Among other Malays, science/technology is more linked to broader questions of food safety and health. The ambiguous question of authority between science/technology, secular government, the marketplace, and religious institutions in modern societies runs through the above discussions. For example, the question of whether halal is or should be linked to health and nutrition is contested. In a broader perspective, these ambiguities challenge the role religion and piety should or should not play in contemporary life among middle-class Malays on the frontier. Hence, many informants claim that halal is not really about religion but mainly about politics and business. However, my study shows that morality is always somehow evoked when discussing modern halal. Zurina, who can be said to belong to a more fastidious register of Malays, makes clear that "for me halal shows how concerned you are being a Muslim, if you are just being a Muslim by name, but not practicing it, so you are the one who should answer to God afterwards." Alina expresses the same ideas, namely, that "you can say that generally speaking the person that is concerned with halal is more religious in anything." In opposition to these sentiments, Fatimah points out that

> I don't think halal is a good way to judge a person, not at all; it is not even an indicator. You can be a practicing Muslim, but you could do other things, which would hurt other people. If they want to be a good Muslim they don't need to show it. Only God knows.

This form of contestation also runs through many of the above discussions of science, food scares, excess, and kosher/vegetarianism, on
the one hand, and halal, on the other.

Miller writes that

> ethics have become extremely diffused across many different issues.
> As a result, the various strands of altruism, taste, self-interest, and so
> forth are so deeply interwoven within the same sentence. As a result,
> the other side to the coin of a general feeling of guilt is a general goal
> that takes the form of being "good" and "doing one's bit."...follow-
> ing a religious rule may become seamlessly integrated into a worry
> about pesticides and making sure that your child has the work disci-
> pline considered appropriate to the better class of primary school. It is
> all part of being "good" and "doing one's bit." (2001: 123)

Many of the issues explored in this chapter were indeed interwoven
within the same sentence when I was discussing these with Malays in
London. However, the aspect of aesthetics informed many of these
discussions and sentences as it were. Although proper halal understanding and practice are contested, these middle-class Malays qualify
as an aesthetic community that generates moral conflicts about the
legitimacy of aesthetic forms or of a morality that rejects these valo-
rized forms.

Conclusion

Five overarching themes have permeated discussions throughout this book: the politics of the national, diasporic identity, and ethnicity; economics in relation to Islam and Malaysia's role in the global market for religious/ethnic commodities; science as a privileged domain highlighting the role of Islam in contemporary, secular settings; authority, particularly linked to the power involved in halal certification embedded in contemporary Malaysian and Islamic institutional discourses and practices; and the multiplicity, ambiguity, and strategizing that arises among middle-class Malays from the above transformations. These themes are all entangled in modern halal, and they effect pluralization of consumer choices and everyday strategies among many Muslim consumers. I shall now conclude my discussion of these overarching themes and bring in a few examples from the preceding chapters with particular reference to informants' understanding and practice of halal. London is a charismatic entity with a marketplace in which the commercial exchangeability of objects, attributes, and skills produces charisma, that is, the proliferation of halal is a good example of a particular type of urban exchangeability that is imbricated in the mundane practices of everyday shopping. Simultaneously, London is a global halal frontier on which questions of politics, economics, science, and authority interpenetrate in a dynamic manner.

First, the politics of the national, diasporic identity, and ethnicity are important themes that have informed discussions in previous chapters. Many middle-class Malays acknowledge that they come from a country or culture where halal is privileged as a religious, national, or ethnic signifier. Despite the fact that Malays in London are outside the direct gaze of the Malaysian state, Malay groups seem to some extent to be united or linked through forms of the United Malay National Organisation (UMNO) and the Malaysian state in London. The Malaysian state was actively involved in forging this mobile New Malay middle class in Malaysia. In a broader perspective, this class emerged in the interfaces between revivalist Islam, state, and market, and their halal consumption is entangled in evermore-complex webs of political, ethnic, and national significance. Food consumption and its religious, social, and cultural context may be the closest one can come to a core symbol in the everyday lives of middle-class Malays. More specifically, all my informants possessed an extensive knowledge of (halal) food that enabled them to identify proper and healthy practices as a modern and cosmopolitan group of Muslims on the frontier. These Malays were clear about food they preferred and avoided; taste/distinctions; shopping strategies; and economic considerations.

At the same time, halal food is about politics and politics at a distance. An example of this is the way in which the Malaysian state has institutionalized halal since the 1980s. Many of my informants acquired their basic knowledge of halal within the school system in Malaysia, and it is this national type of knowledge that now conditions their halal understanding and practice in London. Abdul, for example, referred to this type of knowledge as a natural part of "a national curriculum" or a "common understanding," and Nazli called this a "general knowledge" or "a syllabus." Narratives about the *Shafi'i* school jurisprudence dominant in Malaysia and the ethnic Chinese other informed halal sentiments. Interestingly, for most informants everyday pragmatism was the order of the day when living abroad and without the imagined safety of state-certified products. For example, many Malays in London will shop for halal in local butcher shops even if they can see no visible form of certification and do not really trust the authority of the halal butcher.

The political points seem to be reinforced when a complexification or delocalization of food supply pluralizes everyday food choice, that is, halal is lifted out of local butcher shops to become part of "world food" ranges in supermarkets and hypermarkets. These products are considered expensive compared with inexpensive, but also more questionable, halal meat in local butcher shops. However, these local butcher shops are often more conveniently located.

Halal has become part of a Malaysian national cuisine that involves political economy at different levels of the social scale, that is, in powerful state and commercial discourses in Malaysia and beyond, halal is promoted as healthy and proper for ethnic Malay Muslims. Examples of this were Malaysian institutions' promotion of halal in London. At the same time, political economy and regulation condition actual halal consumption in that due to EU regulations, Malaysia is not allowed to export (halal) meat products to the European Union and Britain. Globally, food scandals such as the one in Indonesia and 9/11 had a forceful impact on the globalization of halal as a religious market. The article "The Halal Way to Free Trade" in *New Straits Times* (May 11, 2006) in connection with the Malaysia International Halal Showcase (MIHAS) evoked these sentiments. It was also in 2006 that Malaysia was represented at the World Food Market (WFM) in London for the first time.

Moreover, developments in Malaysia as a sending country impacts on halal among the Malays in London. For example, halalization in Malaysia developed in the interfaces between Islamic revivalism, state responsiveness, economic growth, ethnicity vis-à-vis the Chinese, and the emerging Malay Muslim middle class. All of this is essential to understand Malay's halal consumption in contemporary London.

The vision to forge a Malaysian halal cuisine has fused with the way in which the state has institutionalized and regulated halal in Malaysia. The dual focus on halal and a Malaysian national cuisine meets in the spaces of the Malaysian halal restaurants in London. One register of my informants is fastidious about halal when eating out. Alina and Zurina, for example, are not only fastidious about halal meat in this respect but also stress the significance of proper certification and handling of halal as well as the ethnicity of the restaurant owner and staff. The second register, Binsar and Abdul, for example, is more pragmatic about the practice of halal space. In essence, these middle-class Malays trust the sellers of halal in "good faith." However, even the more fastidious register of Muslim consumers recognizes that in connection with socializing or work, their halal requirements when eating out cannot fully be met. In general, many of these Malays are relatively pragmatic about halal understanding and practice in a diasporic context.

The Malays are a particular aesthetic community on the frontier, and halal always intertwines the aesthetic and the moral simultaneously, that is, even the most pragmatic or relaxed Malays must negotiate the current proliferation of halal in the material world and in discourse in their everyday lives.

A second theme is economics in relation to Islam and Malaysia's role in the global market for religious/ethnic commodities. Economically, Malaysia has sustained rapid development within the past three decades during which the meaning of Islam has become evermore contested. To preempt the *dakwah* or revivalist Islamic confrontations, the state aggressively engaged in a reconceptualization of consumption that envisions the amalgamation of Malay ethnicity, consumption practices, and Islam. This project is intensifying in the context of economic growth and globalization. The nationalization of Islam means the increased centrality of Islam as a national and ethnic signifier in Malaysia. This nationalization of Islam has initiated a broader fascination with the proper and correct "Islamic way of life," for instance, consuming specific halal goods, which are seen to have a beneficial impact on domains such as family, community, and nation.

Halal in a country such as Malaysia cannot be divorced from economic growth, the emergence of large groups of Malay Muslim middle-class consumers, and centralized state incentives to strengthen halal production, trade, and consumption. Even among the most pragmatic middle-class Malays in London, Malaysian state-certified halal is evoked as a form of shopping for the state or patriotic consumption. For example, Abdul, who can be considered relaxed about halal, acknowledged that Malaysia should make the most of this "untapped" market. What is more, bureaucratically certified halal by the ethnicized state fuels visions and efforts to develop and control the halal market as an economic, religious, and political strategy.

Now capitalism is adjusting to the recent requirements of a growing number of Muslims, and the Islamic market is expanding rapidly. Consequently, in the new millennium, halal also signifies a type of globalized religious market that covers new types of commodities and services. These new commodities (e.g., candy and drinks) were present at the WFM in London.

The proliferation of halal among the Malays in London sits uneasily between an economic dimension linked to investment and trade (the Malaysian vision to become a world leader in halal and the globalization of a Malaysian national halal cuisine) and a future aspect to a large extent nourished by political and Islamic diasporic aspirations. Simultaneously, on the one hand, global capitalism is making peace with cultural diversity (halal is being recognized by multinational companies), and on the other hand, halal is important in identifying different groups of people as aesthetic/moral communities. Hence, halal proliferates in the interfaces between the politics of and markets for modern Muslim identities. Muslim consumers on the frontier are faced with divergent forms of economic reality or rationality, that is, local halal butchers, supermarkets/hypermarkets, and nations (Malaysia, Singapore, and Thailand all have "national" forms of halal certification and logos) with visions to proliferate halal as a global religious market.

A third theme relates to how the privileged position of science in a contemporary and secular setting such as London affects the role of Islam. The sanitization of halal in the modern scientific world pinpoints that halal sits uneasily in and between a plethora of powerful scientific, religious, and political discourses that often overlap. Although meat is the primary type of halal commodity, halal expands into other types of products as well as services and handling. Meat is synonymous with "real" food, and it is eaten on a daily basis by all my informants, but at the same time, it is mostly particular types of meat that are considered problematic with respect to halal and subjected to a range of sentiments and scares, personal, national, and global in scope. The question of whether halal is healthier or not is contested among middle-class Malays. Hence, among my informants, the problem in much discourse about science and halal is that science is seen as part of the solution and the problem.

In general, women compared with men are more fastidious about halal. However, Malay men in London are equally knowledgeable of halal. Members of the new generation of entrepreneurial Malays linked to the Malaysian state—global middle-class New Malays who are highly educated with a "we can" mentality compared with previous generations of "ordinary Malays"—have, most of all, been exposed to the powerful halal discourses. All of this has heightened the awareness of taste, lifestyle, and religion of the younger generation of the middle class to which most of my informants belong.

The proliferation and sanitization of halal in the material world and in discourse increasingly makes it more complex for informants such as Murni and Altaf to practice the "benefit of the doubt" with regard to halal—the notion that "as long as you don't know it's alright, but once the doubtfulness enters your mind, you are not supposed to eat any more" is being subverted when powerful halal discourses demand that Muslim consumers cannot simply assume that their food is halal and that certainty in the form of certification and "scientific" evidence is required as a standard.

A fourth theme is authority, particularly linked to the power involved in halal certification embedded in contemporary Malaysian and Islamic institutional discourses and practices. In a broader perspective, these ambiguities challenge the role religion and piety should or should not play in contemporary life among middle-class Malays on the frontier. Hence, many informants often claim that halal is not really about religion but mainly about politics and business. What was discussed as "secular food" in Britain is a sign of the state's unwillingness or incapacity to recognize the demands of religious consumers. Islamic organizations in Britain claim authority through and compete over halal in the interfaces between expanding markets, the secular, and the rights and demands of Muslim consumers, and it is in this context that Malay diasporic groups consume and negotiate halal. The state in Britain has virtually no authority to inspect, certify, or standardize halal. In the eyes of many of my informants, this leaves consumers unprotected against growing commercial interest in halal. At the same time, some of these middle-class Malays feel that when the state or authoritative religious institutions are not involved, this leaves halal open to excessive commercialization. This impotence of the state is reinforced, as more and more products appear in this expanding market in which both Islamic organizations and commercial interests compete over standards and certification in the margins of the secular state.

Halal in a multitude of commoditized forms is premised on complex understandings and practices of certification. One group of Malays is relatively strict about properly certified halal. They are often interested in the certification of not only meat but also a whole range of other products. In this way, they support the current proliferation of halal. Furthermore, among this register of modern Muslim consumers, halal is not an individualized choice in everyday life but a religious injunction that should inspire a particular form of Muslim lifestyle. Another group of Malay consumers either reluctantly accepts the importance of halal and its certification or simply rejects it as a material, and therefore shallow, display of belief that is unnecessary in their everyday lives. Logos help to personalize halal exchange or transaction, that is, ideally the producer, trader, and consumer all share the symbolic content of the halal logo. Certifying bodies not only claim authority in these transactions but also try to instill in consumers the naturalness and reasonableness of the instituted rules. Advertising these goods can be said to contain religious and totemic dimensions that bring out its culturally potent force. At the same time, halal logos attach political and moral messages to commodities. These systems of certification have grown considerably, but the diversity of these systems the consumers are faced with. At major halal events such as MIHAS and the WFM in London, certification was a major issue of contestation, and it thus constituted a frontier on which widely different ideas and practices of halal met.

The fifth theme has to do with the ultimate complexity and contestation that grow out of the empirical material and point to global halal and global marketing more generally. In each of the previous discussions on "the secular," certification, space, and sanitization, confusion about proper halal consumption on the frontier has been a driving force. Much of this confusion seems to arise because modern halal is not so much about face-to-face relations and participation in a local community but rather about state discourses, institutional certification practices, and science. Halal understandings and practices among informants suggest a religious and ethnic identity that to a large extent is impersonal and technological in nature. In effect, halal has been lifted out of not only local halal butcher shops but also the domain of traditional religious authority. Many Malay middle-class consumers are confused about the moral implications of an expanding halal market, that is, the seemingly boundless expansion of halal and its certification into ever more commodities is seen as excessive and unnecessary. An example of this was crockery (that allegedly could contain crushed bones from pigs), which most informants considered unimportant from a halal perspective. However, all my informants are aware that halal evokes a whole range of moral, political, or patriotic sentiments that are formative of individual, group, and national identities. Consequently, even the most pragmatic Malays acknowledge that a whole range of powerful discourses and practices conditions modern forms of halal.

Even while facing the multiplicity and ambiguity in an expanding religious market, these Muslim consumers are able to forge lives that they understand to be moral, pious, modern, and legitimate within the larger context of British society. While acting in this context requires constant and shifting engagements as well as everyday strategizing, these middle-class Malays are in no way immobilized by "confusion," that is, their understanding and practice of halal is compatible with the ability to actively live as singular and moral persons.

Notes

1 The Halal Frontier

1. The Halal Industry Development Corporation (HDC) was established on September 18, 2006. Its main purpose was to take over JAKIM's responsibilities and
   co-ordinate the overall development of the industry with its main focus being the development of Halal standards, audit and certification, capacity building for Halal products and services as well as to promote and facilitate growth and participation of Malaysian companies in the global Halal market. (www.hdcglobal.com)

2. These four prohibitions parallel those of *kashrut* (Jewish dietary law), which includes a number of additional prohibitions (e.g., many marine species). Compared to halal, kosher requirements have a longer history of systematic institutionalization, certification, and standardization.

3. For a more elaborate discussion of the relationship between religion, science, and markets, see Fischer (2008c).

2 Halal and Malay Middle-Class Mobility in Malaysia

1. In part, this chapter is based on material first published in my monograph (Fischer 2008a), *Proper Islamic Consumption,* published by NIAS Press. I am grateful for NIAS Press giving permission to use this material.

2. SIRIM is an acronym for Malaysian Institute of Industrial Research and Standards.

3. Khazanah Nasional is the
   investment holding arm of the Government of Malaysia and is empowered as the Government's strategic investor in new industries and markets. As trustees to the nation's commercial assets, our main objective is to promote economic growth and make strategic investments on behalf of the Government which would contribute towards nation building. Khazanah is also tasked to nurture the development of selected strategic

industries in Malaysia with the aim of pursuing the nation's long-term economic interests. Khazanah has investments in over 50 major companies, both in Malaysia and abroad, and our companies are involved in a broad spectrum of industries. Khazanah is also the key agency mandated to drive shareholder value creation, efficiency gains and enhance corporate governance in companies controlled by the government, commonly known as Government-Linked Companies, or GLCs. (www.khazanah.com.my)

3   Between Halal and the Secular in London

1. This chapter is a revised version of my article "Feeding Secularism: Consuming Halal among the Malays in London" (Fischer 2009b) in the journal *Diaspora* 18(1): 275–297. This journal is published by University of Toronto Press, and I am grateful for the permission given to use this material.
2. For a discussion of a comparable organization in a French context called *À Votre Service*, "At Your Service," see Bowen (2010).
3. For a more detailed discussion of religious slaughter in a European perspective see Bergeaud-Blackler (2004, 2007).
4. The Food Standards Agency (www.food.gov.uk) is an independent government department established in 2000 to protect the public's health and consumer interests in relation to food.

4   The Other Side of the Logo

1. This chapter is a revised version of my chapter "The Other Side of the Logo: The Global Halal Market in London" (Fischer 2009c) taken from the volume *The New Cultures of Food: Marketing Opportunities from Ethnic, Religious and Cultural Diversity* published by Gower. I am grateful to Gower for giving permission to use this material.

5   Urban Halal Landscapes

1. This chapter is a revised version of my chapter "Halal, Haram or What? Creating Muslim Space in London" (Fischer 2009d) taken from the edited volume *Muslim Societies in the Age of Mass Consumption: Politics, Religion and Identity between the Local and the Global* published by Cambridge Scholars Publishing. This material is published with the permission of Cambridge Scholars Publishing.
2. See, for example, Lefebvre (1992).

6   Halal Sanitized

1. This chapter is a revised version of my article (Fischer 2010) "Halal Sanitised: Health and Science in a Globalised Religious Market" in

Notes

1 The Halal Frontier

1. The Halal Industry Development Corporation (HDC) was established on September 18, 2006. Its main purpose was to take over JAKIM's responsibilities and

   > co-ordinate the overall development of the industry with its main focus being the development of Halal standards, audit and certification, capacity building for Halal products and services as well as to promote and facilitate growth and participation of Malaysian companies in the global Halal market. (www.hdcglobal.com)

2. These four prohibitions parallel those of *kashrut* (Jewish dietary law), which includes a number of additional prohibitions (e.g., many marine species). Compared to halal, kosher requirements have a longer history of systematic institutionalization, certification, and standardization.

3. For a more elaborate discussion of the relationship between religion, science, and markets, see Fischer (2008c).

2 Halal and Malay Middle-Class Mobility in Malaysia

1. In part, this chapter is based on material first published in my monograph (Fischer 2008a), *Proper Islamic Consumption,* published by NIAS Press. I am grateful for NIAS Press giving permission to use this material.

2. SIRIM is an acronym for Malaysian Institute of Industrial Research and Standards.

3. Khazanah Nasional is the

   > investment holding arm of the Government of Malaysia and is empowered as the Government's strategic investor in new industries and markets. As trustees to the nation's commercial assets, our main objective is to promote economic growth and make strategic investments on behalf of the Government which would contribute towards nation building. Khazanah is also tasked to nurture the development of selected strategic

industries in Malaysia with the aim of pursuing the nation's long-term economic interests. Khazanah has investments in over 50 major companies, both in Malaysia and abroad, and our companies are involved in a broad spectrum of industries. Khazanah is also the key agency mandated to drive shareholder value creation, efficiency gains and enhance corporate governance in companies controlled by the government, commonly known as Government-Linked Companies, or GLCs. (www.khazanah.com.my)

3   Between Halal and the Secular in London

1. This chapter is a revised version of my article "Feeding Secularism: Consuming Halal among the Malays in London" (Fischer 2009b) in the journal *Diaspora* 18(1): 275–297. This journal is published by University of Toronto Press, and I am grateful for the permission given to use this material.
2. For a discussion of a comparable organization in a French context called *À Votre Service*, "At Your Service," see Bowen (2010).
3. For a more detailed discussion of religious slaughter in a European perspective see Bergeaud-Blackler (2004, 2007).
4. The Food Standards Agency (www.food.gov.uk) is an independent government department established in 2000 to protect the public's health and consumer interests in relation to food.

4   The Other Side of the Logo

1. This chapter is a revised version of my chapter "The Other Side of the Logo: The Global Halal Market in London" (Fischer 2009c) taken from the volume *The New Cultures of Food: Marketing Opportunities from Ethnic, Religious and Cultural Diversity* published by Gower. I am grateful to Gower for giving permission to use this material.

5   Urban Halal Landscapes

1. This chapter is a revised version of my chapter "Halal, Haram or What? Creating Muslim Space in London" (Fischer 2009d) taken from the edited volume *Muslim Societies in the Age of Mass Consumption: Politics, Religion and Identity between the Local and the Global* published by Cambridge Scholars Publishing. This material is published with the permission of Cambridge Scholars Publishing.
2. See, for example, Lefebvre (1992).

6   Halal Sanitized

1. This chapter is a revised version of my article (Fischer 2010) "Halal Sanitised: Health and Science in a Globalised Religious Market" in

the journal *Tidsskrift for Islamforskning* (4)1: 24–47. This journal is published by Forum for Islamforskning, and I am grateful for permission to use this material.

2. For a more elaborate discussion of the relationship between religion, science, and markets, see Fischer 2008c.

3. More recent literature on migration shopping explores how modern and globalized forms of consumer capitalism have generated the growth of ethnic and "roots" celebrations. In the United States from the 1970s onward, for example, companies started to turn away from mass advertising campaigns to focus on segmented marketing approaches and migrant shopping in particular. In migration shopping, academic ideas about multiculturalism in modern societies fused with the interests of the business sector. Thus, migrant groups were targeted as essential segments of modern consumers who to a large extent construct individual and group ethnic identities through their shopping. In the United States, such migrant shopping campaigns have targeted Jews, Irish-Americans, Hispanics, and more recently Muslims, for example (Halter 2000).

4. For a more detailed ethnography on kosher, see Buckster (1999).

5. See, for example, the organization Orthodox Union's website (http://www.oukosher.org/index.php/).

6. For further perspectives on Islamic banking, see Haron (1997), Kuran (1995, 1997), and Maurer (2005).

Bibliography

Abbas, Tahir. 2005. *Muslim Britain: Communities under Pressure*. London: Zed Books.

Ackerman, Susan E., and Lee, Raymond L. M. 1997. *Sacred Tensions. Modernity and Religious Transformation in Malaysia*. Columbia: University of South Carolina Press.

Agriculture and Agri-Food Canada. 2006. *Halal Food Products Market Report*. Ottawa, ON: Agriculture and Agri-Food Canada.

Ahmed, Allam. 2008. Marketing of Halal Meat in the United Kingdom. *British Food Journal* 110 (7): 655–670.

Anderson, Eugene N. 2007. Malaysian Foodways: Confluence and Separation. *Ecology of Food and Nutrition* 46: 205–219.

Ansari, Humayun. 2004. *The Infidel Within. Muslims in Britain since 1800*. London: Hurst & Company.

Appadurai, Arjun. 1988. How to Make a National Cuisine: Cookbooks in Contemporary India. *Comparative Studies in Society and History* 30 (1): 3–24.

———. 1999. Introduction. Commodities and the Politics of Value. In *The Social Life of Things. Commodities in Cultural Perspective*, edited by Arjun Appadurai, pp. 3–63. Cambridge: Cambridge University Press.

Asad, Talal. 2003. *Formations of the Secular. Christianity, Islam, Modernity*. Stanford: Stanford University Press.

Azmi, Jumaatun. 2003a. *Halal Food: A Guide to Good Eating—Kuala Lumpur*. Kuala Lumpur: KasehDia Sdn. Bhd.

———. 2003b. *Halal Food: A Guide to Good Eating—London*. Kuala Lumpur: KasehDia Sdn. Bhd.

Badawi, Abdullah Ahmad. 2006. *Islam Hadhari. A Model Approach for Development and Progress*. Petaling Jaya: MPH Publishing Sdn Bhd.

Bakar, Osman. 2008. Malaysian Islam in the Twenty-First Century: The Promise of a Democratic Transformation? In *Asian Islam in the 21ˢᵗ Century*, edited by John L. Esposito, John O. Voll and Osman Bakar, pp. 81–108. Oxford: Oxford University Press.

Barthes, Roland. 1975. Towards a Psychosociology of Contemporary Food Consumption. In *European Diet from Pre-Industrial to Modern Times*, edited by Elborg Foster and Robert Foster, pp. 166–173. New York: Harper & Row.

Bauman, Gerd. 1996. *Contesting Culture. Discourses of Identity in Multi-Ethnic London.* Cambridge: Cambridge University Press.

Bennett, Lance W., and Lagos, Taso. 2007. Logo Logic: The Ups and Downs of Branded Political Communication. *The ANNALS of the American Academy of Political and Social Science* 611: 193–206.

Bergeaud-Blackler, Florence. 2004. Social Definitions of *Halal* Quality: The Case of Maghrebi Muslims in France. In *Qualities of Food*, edited by Mark Harvey, Andrew McMeekin and Alan Warde, pp. 94–107. Manchester and New York: Manchester University Press.

———. 2007. New Challenges for Islamic Ritual Slaughter: A European Perspective. *Journal of Ethnic and Migration Studies* 33 (6): 965–980.

BERNAMA (Malaysian National News Agency). 2006. No Need to Review PSD Scholarship Award System. June 29.

Berry, Andrew. 2001. *Political Machines.* London and New York: Athlone Press.

Bourdieu, Pierre. 1984. *Distinction. A Social Critique of the Judgement of Taste.* London: Routledge.

Bowen, John R. 2004. Beyond Migration: Islam as a Transnational Public Space. *Journal of Ethnic and Migration Studies* 30 (5): 879–894.

———. 2010. *Can Islam be French? Pluralism and Pragmatism in a Secularist State.* Princeton, NJ, and Oxford: Princeton University Press.

Bradby, Hannah. 1997. Health, Eating and Heart Attacks. In *Food, Health and Identity*, edited by Pat Caplan, pp. 213–233. London and New York: Routledge.

Brown, Simon, and Saunders, Steven. 1999. *Feng Shui Food: Create Great Looking, Great Tasting Food That Will Revolutionize Your Meals and Revitalize Your Life.* New York: Thorsons.

Brunsson, Nils, and Jakobsson, Bengt. 2000. *A World of Standards.* Oxford and New York: Oxford University Press.

Buckster, Andrew. 1999. Keeping Kosher: Eating and Social Identity Among the Jews of Denmark. *Ethnology* 38 (3): 191–209.

Bunnell, Tim. 2007. Post-Maritime Transnationalization: Malay Seafarers in Liverpool. *Global Networks* 7 (4): 412–429.

Burnett, John. 1966. *Plenty and Want. A Social History of Diet in England from 1815 to the Present Day.* London: Thomas Nelson and Sons Ltd.

Busch, Lawrence. 2004. Grades and Standards in the Social Construction of Safe Food. In *The Politics of Food*, edited by Marianne E. Lien and Brigitte Nerlich, pp. 163–178. Oxford and New York: Berg.

Caplan, Pat. 1997. Approaches to the Study of Food, Health and Identity. In *Food, Health and Identity*, edited by Pat Caplan, pp. 1–31. London and New York: Routledge.

Caplan, Pat, Keane, Anne, Willets, Anna and Williams, Janice. 1998. Studying Food Choice in its Social and Cultural Contexts: Approaches from a Social Anthropological Perspective. In *The Nation's Diet. The Social Science of Food Choice*, edited by Anne Murcott, pp. 168–196. London: Longman.

Caplan, Pat. 2000. "Eating British Beef with Confidence:" A Consideration of Consumers' Responses to BSE in Britain. In *Risk Revisited*, edited by Pat Caplan, pp. 184–203. London, Sterling and Virginia: Pluto Press.

Carsten, Janet, and Hugh-Jones, Stephen. 1995. Introduction: About the House. Lévi-Strauss and Beyond. In *About the House. Lévi-Strauss and Beyond*, edited by Janet Carsten and Stephen Hugh-Jones, pp. 1–46. Cambridge: Cambridge University Press.

Castles, Stephen, and Miller, Mark J. 2009. *The Age of Migration. Third Edition*. New York and London: Palgrave Macmillan.

Charlton, Roger, and Kaye, Ronald. 1985. The Politics of Religious Slaughter: An Ethno-Religious Case Study. *New Community* XII (3): 490–502.

Chawk, Ali, and Ayan, Abdullah. 2006. Population Dynamics, Security and Supply of Halal Food. In *Food and Technological Progress. An Islamic Perspective*, edited by Sheikh Mohd Saifuddeen Shaikh Mohd Salleh and Azrina Sobrian, pp. 73–84. Petaling Jaya: MPH Publishing.

Clifford, James. 1994. Diasporas. *Cultural Anthropology* 9 (3): 302–338.

Consumers Association of Penang. 2006. *Halal Haram. A Guide by Consumers Association of Penang*. Penang: Consumers Association of Penang.

Coveney, John. 2000. *Food, Morals and Meaning. The Pleasure and Anxiety of Eating*. London and New York: Routledge.

Das, Veena, and Poole, Deborah. 2004. State and Its Margins: Comparative Ethnographies. In *Anthropology in the Margins of the State*, edited by Veena Das and Deborah Poole, pp. 3–34. Santa Fe: School of American Research Process and Oxford: James Currey.

Daviron, B., and Ponte, S. 2005. *The Coffee Paradox. Global Markets, Commodity Trade and the Elusive Promise of Development*. London and New York: Zed Books.

D'Alisera, Joann. 2001. I Love Islam. Popular Religious Commodities, Sites of Inscription, and Transnational Sierra Leonean Identity. *Journal of Material Culture* 6 (1): 91–110.

de Certeau, Michel. 1984. *The Practice of Everyday Life*. Berkeley: University of California Press.

Delgado, Linda D. 2005. *Halal Food, Fun and Laughter*. Tempe: Muslim Writers Publishing.

Denny, Frederick Mathewson. 2006. *An Introduction to Islam*. Upper Saddle River, NJ: Pearson Prentice Hall.

Devji, Faisal. 2005. *Landscapes of the Jihad. Militancy, Morality, Modernity*. London: Hurst & Company.

———. 2008. *The Terrorist in Search of Humanity. Militant Islam and Global Politics*. London: Hurst & Company.

Douglas, Mary. 1972. Deciphering a Meal. *Daedalus* 101 (1): 61–81.
———. 1975. *Implicit Meanings*. New York and London: Routledge.
———. 1986. *How Institutions Think*. Syracuse, NY: Syracuse University Press.
———. 2004. *Purity and Danger*. London: Routledge.
Durkheim, Emile. 1995. *The Elementary Forms of Religious Life*. New York: The Free Press.
Eade, John. 2000. *Placing London. From Imperial Capital to Global City*. New York and Oxford: Berghahn Books.
Eliade, Mircea. 1987. *The Sacred and the Profane. The Nature of Religion. The Significance of Religious Myth, Symbolism, and Ritual within Life and Culture*. San Diego, CA, and New York: Harcourt Brace and Company.
Embong, Abdul Rahman. 1998. Social Transformation, the State and the Middle Classes in Post-Independence Malaysia. In *Cultural Contestations. Mediating Identities in a Changing Malaysian Society*, edited by Ibrahim Zawawi, pp. 83–116. London: Asean Academic Press.
Esposito, John L. 1995. *The Oxford Encyclopedia of the Modern Islamic World*. Oxford: Oxford University Press.
———. 2003. *Modernizing Islam: Religion in the Public Sphere in the Middle East and Europe*. New Brunswick: Rutgers University Press.
Evans, Hajj Abdalhamid. 2006. Looking Forward with Hindsight. *The Halal Journal: Business, Lifestyle, Trends*, November–December: 24–25.
Fetzer, Joel S., and Soper, J. Christopher. 2005. *Muslims and the State in Britain, France and Germany*. Cambridge: Cambridge University Press.
Fiddes, Nick. 1991. *Meat. A Natural Symbol*. London and New York: Routledge.
Firth, Raymond W. 1966. *Malay Fishermen: Their Peasant Economy*. New York: The Norton Library.
Fischer, Johan. 2007. Boycott or Buycott? Malay Middle-Class Consumption Post-9/11. *Ethnos* 72 (1): 29–50.
———. 2008a. *Proper Islamic Consumption. Shopping among the Malays in Modern Malaysia*. Copenhagen: NIAS Press.
———. 2008b. Nationalizing Rituals? The Ritual Economy in Malaysia. *Journal of Ritual Studies* (22) 2: 13–22.
———. 2008c. Religion, Science and Markets: Modern Halal Production, Trade and Consumption. *EMBO Reports* 9 (9): 828–883.
———. 2009a. "We Shift the Channel when Mahathir Appears": The Political Internet and Censorship in Malaysia. *Akademika* 75 (1): 43–63.
———. 2009b. Feeding Secularism: Consuming Halal among the Malays in London. *Diaspora* 18 (1): 275–297.
———. 2009c. The Other Side of the Logo: The Global Halal Market in London. In *The New Cultures of Food: Marketing Opportunities from Ethnic, Religious and Cultural Diversity*, edited by Adam Lindgreen and Martin K. Hingley, pp. 73–88. Farnham: Gower Publishing.

———. 2009d. Halal, Haram or What? Creating Muslim Space in London. In *Muslim Societies in the Age of Mass Consumption: Politics, Religion and Identity between the Local and the Global*, edited by Johanna Pink, pp. 3–21. Newcastle upon Tyne: Cambridge Scholars Publishing.

———. 2010. Halal Sanitised: Health and Science in a Globalised Religious Market. *Tidsskrift for Islamforskning* 4 (1): 24–47.

Fischler, Claude. 1988. Food, Self and Identity. *Social Science Information* 27 (2): 275–292.

Funston, John. 2006. Malaysia. In *Voices of Islam in Southeast Asia. A Contemporary Sourcebook*, edited by Greg Fealy and Virginia Hooker, pp. 51–61. Singapore: Institute of Southeast Asian Studies.

Geertz, Clifford. 1968. *Islam Observed. Religious Development in Morocco and Indonesia*. Chicago: University of Chicago Press.

Gillette, Maris Boyd. 2000. *Between Mecca and Beijing. Modernization and Consumption among Urban Chinese Muslims*. Stanford, CA: Stanford University Press.

Goffman, Erving. 1971. *The Presentation of Self in Everyday Life*. London: Penguin Books.

Goody, Jack. 1982. *Cooking, Cuisine and Class. A Study in Comparative Sociology*. Cambridge: Cambridge University Press.

Gottreich, Emily. 2007. *The Mellah of Marrakesh: Jewish and Muslim Space in Morocco's Red City*. Bloomington: Indiana University Press.

Greater London Authority. 2006. *Muslims in London*. London: Greater London Authority.

Green, Sarah, Harvey, Penny, and Knox, Hannah. 2005. Scales of Place and Networks. An Ethnography of the Imperative to Connect through Information and Communications Technologies. *Current Anthropology* 46 (5): 805–826.

Guardian, This Veil Fixation is Doing Muslim Women No Favours, October 19, 2006.

Guardian, Tribunal Dismisses Case of Muslim Woman Ordered Not to Teach in Veil, October 20, 2006.

Guardian, The Veil Controversy, October 21, 2006.

Guardian, Something Fishy in Your Pasta? October 26, 2006.

Guarnizo, Louis E., and Smith, Michael P. 1998. The Locations of Transnationalism. In *Transnationalism from Below*, edited by Louis E. Guarnizo and Michael P. Smith, pp. 3–34. New Brunswick and London: Transaction Publishers.

Halter, M. 2000. *Shopping for Identity. The Marketing of Ethnicity*. New York: Schocken Books.

Hansen, Thomas Blom. 2000. Predicaments of Secularism: Muslim Identities and Politics in Mumbai. *The Journal of the Royal Anthropological Institute* 6 (2): 255–272.

Hansen, Thomas, and Stepputat, Finn. 2001. Introduction. States of Imagination. In *States of Imagination: Ethnographic Explorations of the*

Postcolonial State, edited by Thomas Blom Hansen and Finn Stepputat, pp. 1–41. Durham, NC, and London: Duke University Press.

———. 2005. Introduction. In *Sovereign Bodies. Citizens, Migrants, and States in the Postcolonial World*, edited by Thomas Hansen and Finn Stepputat, pp. 1–38. Princeton, NJ, and Oxford: Princeton University Press.

Hansen, Thomas, and Verkaaik, Oskar. 2009. Introduction—Urban Charisma. On Everyday Mythologies in the City. *Critique of Anthropology* 29 (1): 5–29.

Haron, Sudin. 1997. *Islamic Banking. Rules and Regulations*. Petaling Jaya: Pelanduk Publications.

Harris, Marvin. 1977. *Cannibals and Kings. The Origins of Cultures*. New York: Random House.

———. 1998. *Good to Eat: Riddles of Food and Culture*. Illinois: Waveland Press.

Hart, Keith. 2005. *The Hit Man's Dilemma. Or, Business, Personal and Impersonal*. Chicago, IL: Prickly Paradigm Press.

Hassan, Sita Hasnah, Dann, Stephen, Kamal, Kharil Annuar Mohd, and de Run, Ernest Cyril. 2009. Influence of the Halal Certification Mark in Food Product Advertisements in Malaysia. In *The New Cultures of Food: Marketing Opportunities from Ethnic, Religious and Cultural Diversity*, edited by Adam Lindgreen and Martin K. Hingley, pp. 243–261. Farnham: Gower Publishing.

Isaacs, Ron. 2005. *Kosher Living. It's More Than Just the Food*. San Francisco, CA: John Wiley & Sons, Inc.

Jacobs, Jane M. 1996. *Edge of Empire. Postcolonialism and the City*. New York: Routledge.

James, William. 2002. *Varieties of Religious Experience. A Study in Human Nature*. London and New York: Routledge.

Jomo, K. S., and Cheek, Ahmad Shabery. 1992. Malaysia's Islamic Movements. In *Fragmented Vision. Culture and Politics in Contemporary Malaysia*, edited by Joel S. Kahn and Francis Loh Kok Wah, pp. 162–193. North Sydney: Asian Studies Association of Australia in association with Allen & Unwin.

Jung, Shannon L. 2004. *Food for Life. The Spirituality and Ethics of Eating*. Minneapolis, MN: Fortress Press.

Kaye, Ronald. 1993. The Politics of Religious Slaughter of Animals: Strategies for Ethno-Religious Political Action. *New Community* 19 (2): 251–261.

Kessler, Clive S. 1999. A Malay Diaspora? Another Side of Dr Mahathir's Jewish Problem. *Patterns of Prejudice* 33: 23–42.

Korsmeyer, Carolyn. 1999. *Making Sense of Taste. Food and Philosophy*. Ithaca, NY, and London: Cornell University Press.

Kuran, Timur. 1995. Islamic Economics and the Islamic Subeconomy. *The Journal of Economic Perspectives* 9 (4): 155–173.

———. 1997. The Genesis of Islamic Economics: A Chapter in the Politics of Muslim Identity. *Social Research* 64 (2): 301–338.

Leach, Edmund R. 1960. The Frontiers of "Burma." *Comparative Studies in Society and History* 3: 49–68.

Lee, Raymond L. M. 1993. The Globalization of Religious Markets: International Innovations, Malaysian Consumption. *Sojourn* 8 (1): 35–61.

Lee Sook Ching. 2006. *Cook Malaysian*. Singapore: Marshall Cavendish Cuisine.

Lefebvre, Henri. 1992. *The Production of Space*. Oxford and Malden: Wiley-Blackwell.

Lévi-Strauss, Claude. 1968. *Structural Anthropology*. Vol I. Harmondsworth: Allen Lane, Penguin Press.

Levitt, Peggy. 2001. *The Transnational Villagers*. Berkeley: University of California Press.

Lewis, Philip. 1994. *Islamic Britain. Religion, Politics and Identity among British Muslims: Bradford in the 1990s*. London and New York: I.B. Tauris Publishers.

Lien, Marianne Elisabeth. 2004. The Politics of Food: An Introduction. In *The Politics of Food*, edited by Marianne Lien and Brigitte Nerlich, pp. 1–18. Oxford and New York: Berg.

Mandel, R. 1996. A Place of Their Own: Contesting Spaces and Defining Places in Berlin's Migrant Community. In *Making Muslim Space in North America and Europe*, edited by Barbara D. Metcalf, pp. 147–166. Berkeley, Los Angeles and London: University of California Press.

Manderson, Lenore. 1986a. Introduction. The Anthropology of Food in Oceania and Southeast Asia. In *Shared Wealth and Symbols. Food, Culture and Society in Oceania and Southeast Asia*, edited by Lenore Manderson, pp. 1–25. Cambridge and Melbourne: Cambridge University Press.

———. 1986b. "Food Classification and Restriction in Peninsular Malaysia: Nature, Culture, Hot and Cold?" In *Shared Wealth and Symbol. Food, Culture and Society in Oceania and Southeast Asia*, edited by Lenore Manderson, pp. 127–143. Cambridge and Melbourne: Cambridge University Press.

Mankekar, Purnina. 2004. "India Shopping": Indian Grocery Stores and Transnational Configurations of Belonging. In *The Cultural Politics of Food and Eating. A Reader*, edited by James L. Watson and Melissa Caldwell, pp. 197–214. Oxford: Berg.

Marcus, George E. 1995. Ethnography in/of the World System: The Emergence of Multi-Sited Ethnography. *Annual Review of Anthropology* 24: 95–117.

MATRADE. 2006. *Malaysia. Exporters of Halal Products*. Kuala Lumpur: MATRADE.

Maurer, Bill. 2005. *Mutual Life, Limited. Islamic Banking, Alternative Currencies, Lateral Reason*. Princeton, NJ: Princeton University Press.

Mazzarella, William. 2003. *Shoveling Smoke. Advertising and Globalization in Contemporary India*. Durham, NC, and London: Duke University Press.

McGown, Rima B. 1999. *Muslims in the Diaspora: The Somali Communities of London and Toronto*. Toronto, ON: University of Toronto Press.

Metcalf, Barbara D. 1996. Introduction: Sacred Words, Sanctioned Practice, New Communities. In *Making Muslim Space in North America and Europe*, edited by Barbara Metcalf, pp. 1–27. Los Angeles and London: University of California Press.

Miller, Daniel. 2000. Object Domains, Ideology and Interests. In *The Consumer Society Reader*, edited by Martyn J. Lee, pp. 106–124. Oxford: Blackwell.

———. 2001. *The Dialectics of Shopping*. Chicago and London: University of Chicago Press.

Milner, Anthony. 2008. *The Malays*. Malden, Oxford and Chichester: John Wiley & Sons Ltd.

Mitchell, Timothy. 1999. Society, Economy, and the State Effect. In *State/Culture: New Approaches to the State after the Cultural Turn*, edited by George Steinmetz, pp. 76–97. New York: Cornell University Press.

Modood, Tariq. 2005. *Multicultural Politics. Racism, Ethnicity and Muslims in Britain*. Edinburgh: Edinburgh University Press.

Moeran, Brian. 1996. *A Japanese Advertising Agency: An Anthropology of Media and Markets*. London: Routledge.

Mohamad, Mahathir. 1995. Views and Thoughts of Dr Mahathir Mohamad, the Prime Minister of Malaysia. In *Malaysia's Vision 2020*, edited by Ahmad Sarji Abdul Hamid, pp. 1–51. Kelana Jaya: Pelanduk Publications.

Nagata, Judith. 1984. *The Reflowering of Malaysian Islam. Modern Radicals and Their Roots*. Vancouver: University of British Columbia Press.

———. 1994. How to be Islamic without Being an Islamic State. In *Islam, Globalization and Postmodernity*, edited by Akbar S. Ahmed and Donnan Hastings, pp. 63–90. London: Routledge.

Nasir, Kamaludeen Mohamed, Pereira, Alexius A., and Turner, Bryan S. 2009. *Muslims in Singapore. Piety, Politics and Policies*. London and New York: Routledge.

Navaro-Yashin, Yael. 2002. *Faces of the State: Secularism and Public Life in Turkey*. Princeton, NJ: Princeton University Press.

Nestlé. 2010. Bringing Peace of Mind around the World. *Halal Journal* 35 July/August.

New Straits Times, The Halal Way to Free Trade, May 11, 2006.

New Straits Times, SMEs Urged to Boost Networking at International Halal Event, May 13, 2006.

New Straits Times, Halal Showcase Rakes in Deals Worth RM168m, May 18, 2006.

New Straits Times, No Ordinary Ties, May 29, 2009.

Norwawi, Mohd Effendi. 2006. Food Security from the Malaysian Perspective. In *Food and Technological Progress. An Islamic Perspective*, edited by Sheikh Mohd Saifuddeen Shaikh Mohd Salleh and Azrina Sobrian, pp. 1–14. Petaling Jaya: MPH Publishing.

O'Meara, Simon. 2007. *Space and Muslim Life: At the Limits of the Labyrinth of Fez*. London and New York: Routledge.

Ong, Aihwa. 1995. State versus Islam: Malay Families, Women's Bodies, and the Body Politic in Malaysia. In *Bewitching Women, Pious Men. Gender and Body Politics in Southeast Asia*, edited by Aihwa Ong and Michael G. Peletz, pp. 159–194. Berkeley: University of California Press.

——. 1999. *Flexible Citizenship. The Cultural Logics of Transnationality*. Durham, NC: Duke University Press.

Peletz, Michael G. 1997. "Ordinary Muslims" and Muslim Resurgents in Contemporary Malaysia. Notes on an Ambivalent Relationship. In *Islam in an Era of Nation-States. Politics and Religious Revival in Muslim Southeast Asia*, edited by Robert W. Hefner and Patricia Horvatich, pp. 231–273. Honolulu: University of Hawai'i Press.

Pointing, John, Teinaz, Yunes, and Shafi, Shuja. 2008. Illegal Labelling and Sales of Halal Meat and Food Products. *The Journal of Criminal Law* 72 (3): 206–213.

Pollock, Sheldon, et al. 2002. Cosmopolitanisms. In *Cosmopolitanism*, edited by Carol Breckenridge, et al., pp. 1–14. Durham, NC, and London: Duke University.

Riaz, Mian N., and Chaudry, Muhammad M. 2004. *Halal Food Production*. Boca Raton, FL: CRC Press.

Rose, Jacqueline. 1996. *States of Fantasy*. Oxford: Clarendon Press.

Rouse, Carolyn, and Hoskins, Janet. 2004. Purity, Soul Food, and Sunni Islam: Explorations at the Intersection of Consumption and Resistance. *Cultural Anthropology* 19 (2): 226–249.

Roy, Olivier. 2002. *Globalised Islam: The Search for a New Ummah*. London: Hurst & Company.

Sahlins, Marshall. 1972. *Stone Age Economics*. London: Routledge.

Sallah, Sheikh Mohd Saifuddeen Shaikh Mohd, and Sobrian, Azrina. 2006a. *Food and Technological Progress. An Islamic Perspective*. Petaling Jaya: MPH Publishing.

——. 2006b. Editor's Note. In *Food and Technological Progress. An Islamic Perspective*, edited by Sheikh Mohd Saifuddeen Shaikh Mohd Salleh and Azrina Sobrian, pp. ix–xiv. Petaling Jaya: MPH Publishing.

Sassen, Saskia. 2002. *Global Networks, Linked Cities*. New York and London: Routledge.

Scott, James. 1998. *Seeing Like a State. How Certain Schemes to Improve the Human Condition Have Failed*. New Haven, CT, and London: Yale University Press.

Shamsul, A. B. 1994. Religion and Ethnic Politics in Malaysia—the Significance of the Islamic Resurgence Phenomenon. In *Asian Visions of Authority. Religion and the Modern States of East and Southeast Asia*, edited by Charles F. Keyes, Laurel Kendall and Helen Hardacre, pp. 99–116. Honolulu: University of Hawai'i Press.

——. 2001. Beyond 11 September: A Malaysian Response. *Nordic Institute of Asian Studies Newsletter* No. 4, December.

Sheffield, Tricia. 2006. *The Religious Dimensions of Advertising*. New York and Houndmills: Palgrave Macmillan.

Simoons, Frederick J. 1994. *Eat Not This Flesh: Food Avoidances from Prehistory to the Present*. Madison and London: The University of Wisconsin Press.

Sin, Lin. 2009. The Aspiration for Social Distinction: Malaysian Students in a British University. *Studies in Higher Education* 30 (3): 285–299.

Sloane, Patricia. 1999. *Islam, Modernity and Entrepreneurship among the Malays*. Houndmills, Basingstoke, Hampshire: Macmillan Press.

Starrett, Gregory. 1995. The Political Economy of Religious Commodities in Cairo. *American Anthropologist* 97 (1): 51–68.

Sunday Times, Focus: Is It Time to Take God out of the State? October 22, 2006.

Tambiah, Stanley J. 1990. *Magic, Science, Religion, and the Scope of Rationality*. Cambridge: Cambridge University Press.

Tapper, Richard, and Tapper, Nancy. 1986. "Eat This, It'll Do You a Power of Good:" Food and Commensality among Durrani Pashtuns. *American Ethnologist* 13 (1): 62–79.

Taylor, Charles. 1994. The Politics of Recognition. In *Multiculturalism. Examining the Politics of Recognition*, edited by Amy Gutmann, pp. 25–73. Princeton, NJ: Princeton University Press.

The Malaysian High Commission. 2006. *Programme Book*. London: The Malaysian High Commission.

The Star, Introducing Al Jaulah: Travel with Total Peace of Mind, May 2, 2002.

The Star, Halal Market Can be Used to Rally Muslims, May 11, 2006.

The Star, Don't Blame Them, May 13, 2006.

The Star, Mihas a Huge Success, May 18, 2006.

Tirtha, Swami Sadashiva. 2007. *The Ayurveda Encyclopedia: Natural Secrets to Healing, Prevention, and Longevity*. New York: Ayurveda Holistic Center Press.

Travers, Tony. 2004. *The Politics of London. Governing an Ungovernable City*. Houndmills and New York: Palgrave Macmillan.

Tölölyan, Khachig. 2000. Elites and Institutions in the Armenian Transnation. *Diaspora* 9 (1): 107–136.

Vertovec, Steven. 1996. Muslims, the State, and the Public Sphere in Britain. In *Muslim Communities in the New Europe*, edited by Gerd Nonneman, Tim Niblock and Bogdan Szajkowski, pp. 169–186. Reading: Ithaca Press.

Viladesau, Richard. 1999. *Theological Aesthetics. God in Imagination, Beauty and Art*. New York and London: Oxford University Press.

Wallace, Jennifer. 1998. Introduction. In *Consuming Passions. Food in the Age of Anxiety*, edited by Sia Griffiths and Jennifer Wallace, pp. 1–10. Manchester and New York: Mandolin.

Wallerstein, Immanuel. 1991. The Bourgeois(ie) as Concept and Reality. In *Race, Nation, Class. Ambiguous Identities*, edited by Etienne Balibar and Immanuel Wallerstein, pp. 135–152. London: Verso.

Werbner, Pnina. 1996. The Fusion of Identities: Political Passion and the Poetics of Cultural Performance among British Pakistanis. In *The Politics of Cultural Performance*, edited by David Parkin, Lionel Caplan, Humphrey Fisher, pp. 81–100. Oxford and London: Berghahn Books.

———. 2000. Introduction. The Materiality of Diaspora—Between Aesthetic and "Real" Politics. *Diaspora* 9 (1): 5–20.

Wilk, Richard R. 2002. Food and Nationalism: The Origins of "Belizean Food." In *Food Nations. Selling Taste in Consumer Societies*, edited by Warren Belasco and Philip Scranton, pp. 67–89. New York and London: Routledge.

———. 2006. *Home Cooking in the Global Village. Caribbean Food from Buccaneers to Ecotourists*. Oxford and New York: Berg.

Willets, Anna. 1997. "Bacon Sandwiches Got the Better of Me:" Meat-Eating and Vegetarianism in South-East London. In *Food, Health and Identity*, edited by Pat Caplan, pp. 111–130. London and New York: Routledge.

Wilson, C. S. 1981. Food in a Medical System: Prescriptions and Proscriptions in Health and Illness among Malays. In *Food in Perspective*, edited by Alexander Fenton and Trevor M. Owen, pp. 391–400. Edinburgh: John Donald.

World Food Market. 2006. WFM Official Show Guide. London: World Food Market.

Yao, Souchou. 2002. *Confucian Capitalism. Discourse, Practice and the Myth of Chinese Enterprise*. London: Routledge.

———. 2003. After The Malay Dilemma: The Modern Malay Subject and Cultural Logics of "National Cosmopolitanism" in Malaysia. *Sojourn* 18 (2): 201–229.

Zubaida, Sami. 1994. National, Communal and Global Dimensions in Middle Eastern Food Cultures. In *Culinary Cultures of the Middle East*, edited by Richard Tapper and Sami Zubaida, pp. 33–45. London and New York: I. B. Tauris Publishers.

Zukin, Sharon. 2004. *Point of Purchase. How Shopping Changed American Culture*. New York: Routledge.

Index